D1489133

Building Your Leadership Legacy

It's All About Character

Robert C. Carroll

First Edition: November 2017

Printed in the United States of America

ISBN: 978-1-939237-51-4

Library of Congress Control Number: 2017958707

Published by Suncoast Digital Press, Inc.
Sarasota, Florida, USA

Dedication

With wonderful memories and untold love,
to my wife, Betty Sue.

With deep affection and pride,
to my boys and their wives, KC, Julie, Cody, and Jennifer.

With limitless hopes and dreams,
to my grandchildren, Cooper, Owen, and London.

Contents

Foreword

Leadership is happening all around us. From family dinner tables to kindergarten classrooms, from high school soccer fields to corporate boardrooms and assembly lines, from military basic training grounds and distant battlefields to the cockpits and cabins of complex modern aircraft, from religious leaders to elected officials, leadership, for better or worse, has profound effects.

When we end up being a part of activities that don't succeed or leave us unsatisfied, we often blame the quality of leadership. But it doesn't have to be that way—not when you have the responsibility to lead, and to help others lead better. The author of this book wants to help you find ways to leave your own leadership legacy. His legacy is this book that offers you the gift of his insights based on his unique range of experiences over a lifetime of learning and leading and teaching others to lead and develop others.

Leadership matters and good character makes good leaders. The author knows that leaders also must be competent in many ways, and is well aware that teaching competencies is the heart of a very large leader development industry and so may not be the best area for a meaningful new contribution to the leadership field. He has chosen instead to focus like a laser on how character affects leadership and how good character can be developed.

Bob Carroll is uniquely qualified to write this book. He spent a full career in the US Army as an infantry officer, learning how to lead and leading soldiers, including in combat. He taught leadership in classrooms at the US Military Academy at West Point during a period in which the US Army had to rethink what good leadership meant following the experience of the Vietnam War.

When the nation decided to abandon conscripted service (the draft) in favor of an all-volunteer military force, that required wholesale reforms in how people were to be led. It took more than a decade of teaching leaders how to lead in new ways. The author was in the thick of this very difficult culture change during assignments in the Pentagon as well as the field Army. After retiring from the Army, he began a career of corporate consulting with leaders in global companies whose bottom line was directly affected by the quality of leadership throughout their organizations and whether these corporate leaders could learn how to develop others as leaders for their organizations.

So this book is the culmination of a lifetime of unique personal, scholarly, and professional experiences centered on learning how to lead better and how to help others learn to do so, too. What you will find as you read on is a challenge to conventional ways of thinking about what leadership is and how it can be learned. There is abundant, even overwhelming, evidence that most of leadership is learned behavior. Some of the best evidence for this is the transformation of the young men and women who every year enter the armed forces as immature teenagers and in only four years become mature participants in the leadership of others. Most are ready to lead small teams or are on the threshold of being competent small-group leaders when they transfer that new leadership potential to college campuses and workplaces at the end of their military service.

Leadership depends on both competency and character. For Bob Carroll, leader development is a special case of human development and it takes a lifetime if one is serious about becoming a leader of character. While important, the more common competency approach to leader development can attempt to cover an almost endless number of potentially relevant competencies, raising the question of which competencies are the most important. This approach also risks turning out leadership technicians who are like mechanics, trained to read the instruction book in hopes of then being able to fix specific types of problems such as "decision making" or "leading change." But the best leaders may be more like creative artists who are able to assess novel situations and connect adaptively with the kaleidoscopic nature of human beings whom they seek to influence to strive together to do something that matters to both the leader and the led.

A very big and important part of what makes leaders effective is their character, not just their competencies or "skill sets." The author believes, along with many other scholars and especially people who are or have been leaders, that good character is central to leading well. *The purpose of this book* is to show anyone who is interested how to develop their own character.

Leadership is both competency and character but character is not well understood; how to develop it even less well understood. Because much less is known about character development, there are far fewer resources available to you if you want to learn about character and how to strengthen yours. Perhaps the main reason that character development is not emphasized nearly enough is that it cannot be strengthened or acquired by traditional classroom experiences and is rarely even taught there. So the author offers you a different way of teaching and learning if you choose to try out what you will find here. In your own teaching and coaching, this approach may require you to engage people in less traditional places than college or corporate classrooms.

Bob Carroll has a clear, simple definition of leadership: *influencing others to do something.* He rejects the notion of coercion and asks us to consider how leaders can get others to accept their influence willingly. The fundamental factor in that regard is the establishment of trust in the leader. Without trust there is a much lower limit on what is possible as leaders attempt to influence others "to do something." *The manifestation of character in the leader is the central ingredient when followers decide to trust a leader.*

The character of leaders is much broader than ethics and morality. It includes character traits such as drive, stamina, or grit. For example, some people just don't give up easily, or at all. Such leaders are usually much more effective at getting others to persevere at a difficult task than those who don't work hard or give up easily when adversity enters the picture. Another useful character trait that could be cultivated is openness—the willingness to listen to others, learn from them, and even change direction based on input from team members.

Equally important is the case of leaders who have bad or negative character traits because people are usually, but not always, repelled by and reject leaders with bad character. Even our armed forces must deal with a not insignificant number of leaders who behave in ways that have been called "toxic leadership." Every year a few senior leaders with decades of experience begin to reveal the "dark side" of their character in very destructive and harmful ways and often must be terminated. Similar problems surface in corporate America, too.

One of the worst selection errors an organization can make is to hire a sociopath for a significant leadership role. These are people without empathy, shame, or guilt who are vain and self-centered, lack judgment, and avoid responsibility for their own actions. They lack many crucial good character traits. Yet they can also be superficially charming, enabling them to get hired and attract followers in the short run. Most people aren't sociopaths. But most people do have at least one negative character trait that can reduce their acceptance by others as a leader. Even more harmful, according to research, having two or more negative character traits can cause leaders to fail and leave a trail of damage that can include valued employees jumping ship to get away from such a leader. So Carroll cautions us to seek not just to acquire and strengthen good character but also to get rid of bad or negative character traits that can undermine trust when we try to lead others.

Character has been defined in many ways and there is no agreement on a universal definition of good character. That doesn't bother Bob Carroll one bit as he will show you that what matters is for each of us to define the character traits we want or think we need to strengthen or acquire. *Those are the only ones you are likely to try to change or develop.* That personal source of motivation is needed to start and sustain the difficult work of defining and then assessing your own character traits and helping others in a caring way to do the same. Which ones are important can only be answered by you after careful reflection. The author describes a potentially powerful method for you to use if you decide to get to work on your own list of desired character traits.

Some have suggested that leadership is either just a matter of having "the right stuff" or it is all just "common sense." But that can't be right because good leadership is far too uncommon! Some have even suggested that there is a worldwide shortage of good leaders. *Building Your Leadership Legacy* is a very good book that clearly shows how character is a key component of leadership. It will add value to the field of leadership studies and will be very useful to readers like you who simply want to lead better and ultimately wish to leave your own leadership legacy of many other good leaders you helped to develop.

Howard T. Prince II, PhD
Loyd Hackler Chair in Ethical Leadership
Lyndon B. Johnson School of Public Affairs
The University of Texas at Austin
Brigadier General, USA, Retired

Preface

My wife recently passed away.

Our two wonderful boys strongly encouraged me to write the book I had been talking about for years. They said I had the time now and no excuse. They said I had spent a very fulfilling career with unparalleled experience in the field of leadership: as a practitioner, teacher, and consultant, across both the military and civilian sectors, in the US and abroad.

"Get on with it."

So I took them up on it.

While crafting my wife's eulogy, in a labor of love, I was reminded of the contrast David Brooks makes between a eulogy and a resume.[1] We have all written glowing resumes, addressing the marvelous accomplishments we think might enhance our personal marketability. But people are much more interested in **who we are** than **what we did**. The eulogy is more important than the resume. That insight sparked my approach to this book about leadership.

Ever wonder what people will say about you as a leader? When you leave a job? When you get promoted? When you move on to another company? When you move on in life? Ever wonder what your leadership legacy will be? I decided to approach this topic of leadership from the point of view of **what people think of you** as opposed to **what people think you accomplished.**

For whom am I writing this book?

I am casting a very wide net. I am of the belief that leadership is pervasive, literally everywhere, at all levels, and in every facet of society:

- In an infantry platoon in Afghanistan and in the US Central Command Headquarters in Tampa;

- In the night shift of a McDonald's restaurant in Los Angeles and in the McDonald's CEO suite in Chicago;

- In a high school history classroom in Miami and in the Harvard Business School in Cambridge;

- In a not-for-profit staff meeting in Denver and in the halls of Congress in our Nation's Capital;

- In a girls' soccer practice in Buffalo and in a Chicago Cub's game at Wrigley Field;

- In a dental clinic in Topeka and in the Mayo Clinic operating room in Jacksonville;

- Around the supper table of a family in Seattle and at a State Dinner in the White House.

Leadership from my point of view is pervasive. It occurs at all levels and in all walks of life. It is not just relegated to the top of companies. Leadership is manifested throughout all organizations. Sometimes the leadership is poor, often mediocre, and on occasion wonderful. But it exists whether or not the people doing the leading are aware of it.

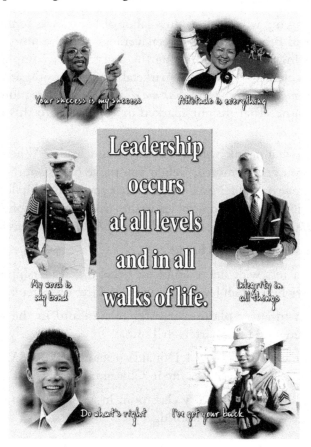

I only know three of these folks: Cadet Tyler Gordon, First Captain, United States Corps of Cadets, on parade; Cheerleader, Ms. Hu Dongmei, Director-General, Beijing Heaven Technology Corporation Ltd., on a visit to West Point; and Staff Sergeant Bob Spenser, A Company, 1st Battalion 503d Infantry, 173d Airborne Brigade, in Vietnam.

This book is written for anyone at any level wishing to be a better leader. It might not make you a great leader, but it surely will make you a better leader. It will significantly improve what people you are leading will say about you when you depart — the job or the earth. It will help you to significantly build your leadership legacy.

The book is also written for those among us who wish to be known for the leaders we develop. I know of many leaders who speak with great pride about the folks who followed in their footsteps and became solid leaders. Speaking of the people he recruited, trained, and propelled on their own careers, one retired friend of mine said that was his greatest legacy. Too often it has been my experience that the development of leaders in organizations of all types is a very low priority. That is a grave disservice to subordinates and to the organization as a whole.

The book is also written for leaders in organizations who wish to develop a cadre of leaders throughout and at all levels of the organization. Therefore it is for the Corporation CEO, organization President, or Human Resources Officer who wishes his or her legacy to be the creation of a superb leadership development system for the entire institution. Not a small task.

Finally, the book is written for professors, instructors, teachers at any institution who wish to enhance markedly the effectiveness of their leadership classes.

Let me take you on a quick walk-through of the chapters:

1. I offer a very basic and workable definition of leadership. It includes anyone leading one or more people anywhere. So it has universal application. But it has a singular focus, **_influencing_** people to do something. The definition of leadership then applies equally to the armed forces and to companies in the private and public sectors. It also applies to every leader at every level. Hence it applies to General Eisenhower with his "Crusade in Europe," to a sales manager of a Hi Tech company, to a foreman in a paper recycling plant, and to the CEO of any Fortune 500 company.

2. In this chapter, I provide a brief but very broad review of what people have written on this subject and how it is being taught. The shelf is huge: it covers a wide array of academic disciplines; scores of memoirs written by folks who are of the opinion that they are leaders exemplar, and a host of self-help books designed to create what Warren Bennis called the "McLeader." This chapter also paints the landscape where this subject is being taught and by whom. I am presenting this survey in order to argue that leadership training is much more widespread than most are aware and that it is mediocre at best. All of this is prelude to my introducing a different (and I believe more productive) approach to leadership.

3. Then I introduce two major themes:

   • Leadership is both competency and character.

   • There are a paltry few programs anywhere that even offer a clue on how to assess and improve the latter.

4. This chapter focuses on the character part of leadership. It is intended to provide you an opportunity and a method to define what kind of leader of character you aspire to be and to embark on a journey to achieve that goal. In a real sense this goal can be the legacy you wish to leave as a leader. Notice my approach is to lay out a method for you to define the kind of character you wish to manifest and to be. This is quite different from others who prescribe character traits necessary for successful leadership. This chapter therefore requires a good bit of reflection on your part. And well worth it.

5. To make your journey successful, I believe you need a way to measure, gain feedback on, and improve your own leadership character. This chapter is devoted to that end. Some argue that character is important but difficult to define and even harder to measure. However, the approach presented here can be extremely effective.

6. The best leaders I have ever known have all prided themselves in recruiting, developing and promoting leaders. This chapter addresses the issue of how to help leaders under your charge become even better leaders. Would you not be intensely proud to have people describe your legacy as one who inspired and developed leadership in subordinates?

7. In this chapter I offer a case study on how West Point does such a magnificent job developing leaders. West Point is considered by many to be the world's premier leadership development institution. And I believe there are lessons to be learned from this case study that are very applicable to you if you are interested in improving your own personal leadership or the leadership throughout your organization.

8. Drawing from the description of West Point, this chapter will help you transfer lessons of leader development to your own company and unique situation. It is obvious that you would not wish to, and in fact could not, create a surrogate academy. But there are principles and techniques that can serve you well.

9. Having taught leadership in a host of different venues, I am very aware of the needs and expectations of students and clients who wish to improve their own leadership. This chapter is written for the leadership professor, instructor or teacher at any level and at any institution. I will offer you some ideas on how to take your game up a significant notch.

10. My final chapter is a heartfelt hope that you will look at leadership from a different light, that you will approach leadership development from a different vantage point, and that you will significantly enhance your own personal leadership legacy.

Safe and productive journey.

Manasota Key, Englewood, Florida

Acknowledgments

To my sons KC and Cody, thank you for your encouragement to launch this project and for your love and support during its execution and beyond.

I send special appreciation to my two consulting partners, Ernie Webb, the best leader I have ever known, and Dennis Alimena, the best leadership coach I have ever known. Watching you two in action inspired me more than any class or book.

I will always be indebted to Howard Prince, a member of my squad when we entered West Point. Howie, you are one of the few who know that I survived "Beast Barracks" only by resorting to an uncontrollable laugh that neutered the ability of the upper class to humiliate me. A true expert in this field, you have been a great source of insight and published resources for me as I wrote this book. And thanks again for writing the foreword.

I wish to express my appreciation to significant teachers over the years who have guided me in my career of working in the field of leadership. At West Point, Major Volney Warner, who later wore four stars, taught me as a cadet a class on the topic, "Group Dynamics." At Northwestern, Sociology Professor Charlie Moskos became my life-long teacher, mentor, and friend. Later at the Military Academy, John Johns and others were instrumental in expanding my approach of teaching leadership using a truly multidisciplinary perspective. At the Harvard Business School, Professor Jay Lorsch greatly broadened my understanding of the field of human resources management. At the Senn-Delaney Leadership Consulting Company, I was given access to executives of companies across many industries and I was taught a process and method of leadership training and teambuilding that is the most effective and powerful I have seen. And I have been fortunate to have had some great bosses to work for and some great people to work with, too numerous to mention.

My heartfelt thanks to you who have read and provided input on my drafts: Jyll Holzman, Andrew Bond, Howard Prince, Bob Phillips, Fred Schaum, Ernie Webb, Dennis Alimena, Lewis Higinbotham, Len Ferraguzzi, Peter Huber, and Bill Regnery. Multiple sets of eyes really helped. Thanks.

And thank you Barbara Dee for your advice and editing, both superb, and for all the help from your team at Suncoast Digital Press, Inc.

Like most books, I close with an acknowledgment that any errors or misstatements belong to me alone. It is particularly appropriate for the author of this book on leadership character to "own it." One aspect of character which is near the top of my list is "accountability." No blame game here.

Bob Carroll

Chapter 1

What is Leadership?

"I can't define leadership, but I know it when I see it."[1]

Let me start by telling you a story about a leader.

The setting for this story is in the military. But this example in no way forecasts that this book is only about leadership in the military. On the contrary this book is about leadership in every aspect of our society. The story is also about a leader fairly low in the organization, which serves to demonstrate that this book is targeted at leadership at all levels of any organization – and that in my view leadership is ubiquitous.

It was a late afternoon in April 1967 in the Iron Triangle of the Republic of Vietnam. As a Rifle Company Commander in the 173d Airborne Brigade, I called three sergeants into my command post to give them instructions for that night. We were to send out three separate, smallish (10-12 men) ambush patrols about two miles in front of our perimeter. The three sergeants took careful notes and studied their maps, as I gave them their mission and guidance using the Army's standard, five-paragraph operations order.

"Questions?"

None.

"Good luck!"

Salutes.

As the three left, one stopped and pulled out of the webbing of his helmet liner a miniature bible. Staff Sergeant Alain Tremblay opened it, read a brief passage, closed it, and then departed to talk to his troops.

That night all three ambushes were activated. My memory is that they all did well with few friendly casualties. From my vantage point, the best led was Tremblay's. I say that was because he was able to quiet his mind, calm

1

his fears, focus on his men and the task at hand, and stay amazingly cool under fire. Soldiers want that in their leaders, I can assure you.

Tremblay was the best leader that day, not because he had previously been a Trappist Monk, one who serves the Lord in contemplative silence, and not because he read from a Christian bible, but because he was able to control his thoughts, hence his behavior. This isn't a story about religious morality. It is about what causes soldiers to trust their leader. And it isn't a story about exceptionally bold or brave leadership. Tremblay did not receive the Medal of Honor. He just did very well what good Non-Commissioned Officers did across Vietnam over many, many years.

Not long after this incident, Tremblay transferred to the 173d Airborne Brigade's elite, Long Range Reconnaissance Patrol Platoon.

He was killed in action on July 7, 1968. *Requiescat in Pace* (**R.I.P.**), good soldier.

Staff Sergeant Alain J. Tremblay, US Army, 1967,
on leave between Vietnam tours, Long Island, NY

I use this story to help define leadership and my approach to it.

Years ago one of my colleagues assembled a list of some one hundred printed definitions of leadership. Recently Harvard's Barbara Kellerman referred to "1500 at last count."[2]

I like the simplicity of Eisenhower's four-part definition.[3] The following is not a quote, but it's close:

> A leader   influences   a person or persons   to do something.

Start with the subject, **"A leader."**

In this case it was Staff Sergeant Tremblay. A leader is not an institution, not a force of nature, not a bureaucracy. A leader is a person, a man or a woman. The word leader is also not confined to high levels of an organization or a nation or to notoriety or history. Leaders exist at all levels and in all walks of life. My own belief is that leadership at the bottom of an organization (the first level of supervision) is more challenging than any other. This is a leadership book that applies to supervisors and CEO's, to coaches and parents, to teachers and politicians. I am not going to center my presentation on historic leaders or heads of governments and large corporations. But the ideas apply to them as well.

Nor will I debate the grand old argument that a leader is born not made, or vice versa. Let us agree that we are all born with a genetic make-up that sets the table for what we become: smart, strong, fast, etc. And that we are all molded by a host of variables after the womb and throughout life: family, schools, community, etc. Suffice it to say leaders develop over their lifetimes. We can't do much about pre-birth; let's focus on how leaders are made after that.

While on this topic, note "leader" is singular. While there are times when leadership is shared, it is more typically one person's role. The Army has a deep tradition of insuring one leader is always in charge. When in doubt, seniority is determined by date of rank; when same date, alphabetically by last name; when same last name, alphabetically by first name.

Such was the case at 7 AM, December 7, 1941, on the north coast of Oahu, Hawaii, for a two-man radar team which spotted a swarm of 50 planes about 137 miles out. Although four years younger than Private George E. Elliot Jr., 23, Private Joseph L. Lockard, 19, the senior of the two, hence the leader, radioed the finding to his headquarters at Ft Shafter, but to little avail. After Pearl Harbor, the younger but senior Private Lockard received the Distinguished Service Medal and was dubbed the "Hero of Pearl Harbor."[4]

There are exceptions to the singularity aspect of leadership: In 1804 Captain Meriwether Lewis gave his close friend and partner Second Lieutenant

William Clark an unauthorized brevet promotion to Captain so the men and the one woman on their famous expedition would see them as equal partners in leadership and in history.

But President Harry Truman's famous desk sign depicts this notion that only one person is in charge:

"The buck stops here."

How frequently we see a leader trying to pass the proverbial buck when something runs amok?

The verb **"influence"** means to move someone via persuasion or example.

Much has been written on the how, when, and why people are influenced. The best overview of this topic I have read is from an article, "The Bases of Social Power" in which French and Raven describe five broad ways to influence.[5]

1. *Reward Power* is any kind of reward the leader is able to offer or provide. It can range from a simple thanks to an excellent rating in a personnel file, a salary increase, attendance at a school, or promotion. One unique example comes from an outstanding Infantry Lieutenant in Vietnam named Larry Payne, who wrote to the parents of each of his soldiers at Christmas saying, "Your son is a fine soldier and I will do everything in my power to get him home safe and sound."

2. *Coercive Power* is the ability to mete out punishment or threaten same. This also can range from a short conversation by the leader to the led either before or after an event, to a bad report in a personnel file to a severe monetary penalty, denial of promotion or termination of employment. Extreme for serious crimes could involve the judicial system. One of the most unique I witnessed was a CEO dealing with an infraction of a senior executive who had compromised his position: "Your pay effective today is cut [$XX,XX], and before you leave tonight I want on my desk a letter of resignation signed but undated which I will execute if this ever happens again."

3. *Legitimate Power* is power provided to a leader by the norms and institutional rules of any organization. A manager has granted authority over the people on any given team. While often there is dotted line authority, meaning more than one boss, the one supervisor is normally the person who sends in the yearly appraisal and recommends any salary increase. I once was in the office of a

President of a Corporation when he got a call from one of his Division Presidents. While I could only hear one side of the conversation, it was easy to tell there was a serious argument going on. With just a touch of sarcasm, the President underscored his legitimate power with a question, "Let me get this straight, do I work for you, or do you work for me?"

4. *Referent Power* is derived from the leader being the type of person someone is naturally attracted to or wants to be like. There is something about the leader that attracts a person and makes that person want to be like the leader. A commonly used term, charisma, falls into this category. Sometimes, the leader "looks the part"; sometimes it is a talent like being smart, creative, or articulate. Often it is because of values and actions that people look up to. One of my heroes at West Point was "the big man on campus," Pete Dawkins, First Captain of the Corps of Cadets, President of his class, Captain of the football team, 1959 Heisman Trophy winner, highest-scoring collegiate defensive hockey player in America, graduated seventh in his class, Rhodes Scholar, and a nice, decent guy. What's not to like?

5. *Expert Power* is when the leader is perceived to have some knowledge related to the task at hand. This could come from education, past experience, or familiarity with a situation. Fundamentally, does the leader know what he or she is doing? It could pertain to a leader not knowing much about a given problem, but being an expert at a process to find out the best course of action. I know of one senior executive who was recruited from an entirely different industry simply because she had a fantastic reputation in marketing. She knew nothing about the products or system of the new company but had great expertise in one area and drew on that for her ability to influence.

What is influenced in this definition has to be **"a person or persons."**

Sergeant Tremblay led an infantry squad of about ten American soldiers. These happened to be very young men who were drafted or volunteered to fight a war little understood or supported by their countrymen. They had to be led on this dangerous night patrol, not managed. You can manage an inventory or a bottom line. But if you are going to lead, according to my definition, it must involve people. For instance, you can't "lead" the launch of a new product;

you "manage" the launch. And you "lead" people to launch the new product.

The distinction between leadership and management is crucial. When you focus on the interaction and interplay between a person who is a leader and the people who are led, it becomes more difficult to describe and almost impossible to measure. The interaction is emotional, sometimes irrational, often energizing, always dynamic and reciprocal, occasionally transformative. It is to my mind the most exhilarating of human endeavors, and it is why I wrote this book.

Finally, the definition needs a clear outcome, namely **"to do something."**

If the people were going to do it anyway, one could argue that the leader did nothing to influence the person or persons. In Sergeant Tremblay's case, the men most likely would have conducted the ambush patrol regardless of his leadership. But they did it better because of his leadership. How they did it was greatly influenced by Sergeant Tremblay.

Hence Staff Sergeant ***Tremblay influenced*** his infantry **squad** to conduct an outstanding ***night ambush patrol***—which is my definition of leadership.

There are a lot of factors around this definition that are omitted for simplicity's sake: the enemy, terrain, weather, competency of the team, past experiences, and luck, just to name a few.

Some argue that military leadership is easier than leadership in the rest of society. There are institutional and legal requirements for members of the military to obey orders. Not only do members of the military take an oath to obey lawful orders, but also they are part of a very hierarchical organization which has a strong autocratic tradition. Followers have to follow orders. Therefore, the job of leadership in the military is easier, say some.

Others argue that leadership is more challenging in the military because those being led could well be wounded or killed. It takes strong and skillful leadership to cause soldiers to ride "Into the jaws of Death, Into the mouth of Hell" as Alfred, Lord Tennyson put it.[6] Added to that threat of life and limb, the leader must order his or her followers to kill other people (the enemy), not the most positive of goals, one could argue. "Anyone who can lead soldiers in battle can lead anyone" is a common refrain. Conclusion: leadership is harder in the military.

Still others see the life and death challenge that the enemy poses as a unifying factor which coalesces the team and encourages compliance with the leader's orders. My own experience is that soldiers in the heat of battle want strong, decisive, and clear leadership more than anything. I personally found leadership in combat easier in this sense than leadership when the bullets were not flying.

While the demands and constraints of the leadership situation are different depending on the setting, be it military or across society, I am of the belief that the same basic elements for successful leadership exist in virtually any scenario. It is only that in combat, unlike most instances, the repercussions of leadership can be life threatening.

So this is a book about leadership in any setting. Leadership in the military will inform but not restrict my approach. My lifelong experience in the US Army and the corporate world has led me to believe that the core elements of leadership are the same across both.

And my approach will not focus on how great the accomplishment, or how historical or powerful the leader. I take this tack in order to include leaders of all levels and kinds into my definition and to invite their interest.

I believe there are few people who are not capable of leadership and most are doing it whether they realize it or not. The real questions are "How are they doing it?" and "How can they improve?" All of them.

All of you.

Chapter 2

How is Leadership Taught?

"More has been written, and less is known about leadership than any other topic in the behavioral sciences."
Warren Bennis[1]

My intent in this book is to present what I hope you will find to be an innovative and extremely helpful approach to leadership. In this chapter, I offer a comprehensive overview of the landscape of leadership as I see it. I believe this survey of teaching leadership is necessary. Otherwise, you will not know in what way my approach is different.

This review includes leadership doctrine (What is being taught?), leadership instruction (Who is teaching it?), and the result (How effective is the teaching?). Perhaps it will confirm what you may already suspect:

- There are a whole lot of folks writing about leadership and teaching it.
- The results of leadership training and education are mediocre at best.

What is being taught?

The first book on leadership I read was in 1962 when I was a senior at West Point taking a course which I believe was the only accredited leadership course in the country at the time. Since then, leadership as a topic has exploded. It is now an immensely popular topic which produces hundreds of books yearly. An Amazon.com query produced 189,000 leadership titles. A Google search came up with 765 million links to leadership.

This seemingly late arrival of leadership to the world of books belies the history of the true body of literature on the topic. A cursory survey of great authors reveals that leadership has been around for a long time. The Ten Commandments are a pretty good example of leadership principles. After Moses came Confucius, Aristotle, Christ, Muhammad, Machiavelli,

Shakespeare, Locke and many others. Even Max Weber, known largely for his concept of "bureaucracy" after studying the organization of the Prussian Army in 1888, also originated the term "charismatic leader."[2] And leadership often gets interwoven with management. Starting in 1911 with Frederick W. Taylor's *The Principles of Scientific Management*, the titles of seminal books speak of the topic of management and the focus on the executive as a manager.[3] Pundits debate whether leadership is an art or a science. What they often are debating is whether it is best to study it using the scientific method or an artistic approach. I choose to side with those who say it is both. There is an abundant body of literature on management. I believe it's because it lends itself better to scientific theory arguably more useful than artistic commentary.

In the 1930's, the human side of management (close to my definition of leadership) became the focus. It started with the Hawthorne Studies, named after a Western Electric factory in Chicago, which focused on worker motivation.[4]

In 1954, two groundbreaking additions to the leadership shelf came from people not normally associated with the term leadership. Known as the father of management, Peter Drucker wrote *The Practice of Management* with a large nod to the concept of leadership.[5] And Abraham Maslow's famous hierarchy of needs pyramid added to the insight of what every person really needs, obviously central to the discussion of leadership.[6]

There has been an effort to use science to observe and describe leadership. Foremost was the Ohio State Leadership Studies which found that to foster goal accomplishment, leaders need to exhibit two types of behaviors, namely "initiating structure" and "showing consideration."[7] Not to be outdone, their football rival, Michigan, made a similar conclusion but substituted "press for production" for "initiating structure." Since that time scholars have had an ongoing debate about whether or not there is a core set of behaviors that cuts across any situation, level, or challenge.

In 1978, James MacGregor Burns brought his history and political science talent to the field with his Pulitzer Prize winning *Leadership*. Burns also introduced the concept that leadership has a singular moral aspect.[8] I will build upon that in later chapters. In 1982, W. Edwards Deming, known for his work during the Total Quality Movement and revered in Japan for his post-war impact there, penned *The fourteen Obligations of Top Management*, very much addressing the idea of leadership.[9] And in 1993, James Garner capped his career of education and government service with a profound work, *On Leadership*.[10]

In 1982, came Peters and Waterman's *In Search of Excellence,* the largest selling text in American history at the time. It heralded a trend of books with case studies at senior levels of leadership. The concept is to showcase one or more top executives exemplifying some fundamental or novel aspect of leadership. Top sellers in this genre are works by Warren Bennis and John Kotter, both prolific and bestselling authors.[11]

There is also a huge segment of the leadership book market called "self-help." It started with the 1936 launch of the very popular *How to Win Friends and Influence People* by Dale Carnegie (still in print, with 14 million copies sold to date).[12] Capping this genre is Stephen Covey's 1989 international bestseller, *The 7 Habits of Highly Effective People.*[13] The magic number seems to be *seven* things to do to be a good leader, although I have read some great books with a list of *four* or *five*, a not-so-bad book with a list of *twenty*, a book I didn't finish with *thirty-one*, and a profound book with just *one—Know Yourself.*

Pause for a minute…can't you imagine some Greek leader in ancient times hiking up the mountain to the shrine of the Oracle of Delphi for some great advice on a perplexing problem? Breathing heavily, he reads the Delphic maxim engraved thereon, "Know Thyself." "Thank you. So helpful!" Tongue in cheek … that edict really is profound, and it is at the core of my approach to leadership.

It's hard to argue that these self-help books are not leadership texts. Even beyond this category of self-help, any biography of a great leader could be classified as a leadership text.

Today, at least in America, every leader of import has one or more biographical or auto-biographical books. And the list of historical biographies is endless.

A recent trend in leadership is to examine bad leadership, looking for what to avoid—sort of the reverse angle approach. The Army has focused on "Toxic Leadership," looking at a small but critical segment of its command structure that brandishes a bullying style, "focused on visible short-term mission accomplishment… [but] unconcerned about, or oblivious to staff or troop morale and/or climate … [and] seen by the majority of subordinates as arrogant, self-serving, inflexible, and petty."[14]

Robert and Joyce Hogan write about the same problem in civilian firms. They study leadership effectiveness from the perspective of "managerial derailment," when leaders "are unable to learn from their past experience ... are extremely self-centered in one way or another ... will serve themselves before they serve others... and continuously erode the trust of their team mates."[15]

We are reminded all too frequently about figures in the public eye, most often at a high level, who commit egregious acts typically causing the demise of their careers and in some cases jail time. There is some data to suggest that culpability is greater near the top: Power breeds an abuse of power.[16] But my view is that leadership malfeasance is equally distributed up and down the organization. I believe both good and bad leadership exist at all levels.

In sum, the domain of books on leadership is immense. It cuts across philosophy, history, sociology, psychology, political science, economics, law, literature, and to a lesser degree, even genetics, psychoanalysis, and neuroscience.

Who is teaching it?

For courses on leadership, too often we think of just colleges and universities, but my analysis reveals a much broader swath of teachers who draw largely from what is published by professors. Those engaged in leadership development are part of a very large enterprise in the US with total revenue estimated at over $14 billion per year.[17]

I have divided this huge industry of leadership teaching into **four categories**:

1. Academia

Paralleling the development of the literature on management was the birth in academia of the modern school of management. The first course on management was taught at the Wharton School of the University of Pennsylvania in 1880. The first advanced degree in business (Master of Science in Commerce) was conferred by the Tuck School of Business at Dartmouth College in 1900. Then came Harvard's Graduate School of Business Management with the first Masters in Business Administration in 1908.[18]

Today in the US this academic field of business management has ballooned to 329 accredited business schools and 6,900 accredited post-secondary institutions and programs. And there is at least one institution which grants a baccalaureate in leadership, the Jepson School of Leadership Studies at the University of Richmond.[19]

At the executive level, Harvard was the first with its 1943 course for senior executives coping with the transformation of our industrial base to support the war effort. It evolved into the elite Advanced Management Program.[20] Now for senior managers beyond college years, executive programs flourish at virtually every university in the country, as well as non-degree granting institutions like the superb Center for Creative Leadership.[21] With his unique brand of wry humor, Warren Bennis described this industry of executive education as "the great training robbery."[22] (Of course, he made a decent living at it, as did I.)

2. Management Consulting Companies

Starting in the 1920's, a management consulting industry was spawned largely by academia. Not unlike the literature review above, this management consulting industry is also very large, diverse, and somewhat hard to define.

The total industry is estimated at over $200 billion, with the most prestigious being McKinsey, Boston Consulting Group, Bain, Deloitte Consulting, and Booz Allen Hamilton.[23] I believe the total number of firms in this category to be huge, considering there are so many very small firms, some with just one person often in transition between jobs. The result is an extremely large cadre of consultants. Derisive jokes abound:

> **"A consultant first asks the client to borrow a watch;**
> **then the consultant tells the client the time;**
> **then the consultant keeps the watch."**

Closely allied with management consultancies are accounting firms, whose beginnings go back to the mid-1850's in London. The accounting firms are mentioned because today they often have leadership and management consulting practices. To be fair, all these consulting firms sell services across accounting, strategy, operations, and technology, many with expertise in specific industries. But many of these firms, especially the larger ones, include leadership as well. For instance, accounting giant PricewaterhouseCoopers, listed as No. 5 on Forbes list of private companies has offerings in leadership and management.[24] A retired accountant told me, "Leadership advice was a very large part of my practice. Once I had the rapport, it was a natural next step."

3. Training Companies

These companies sell off-the-shelf courses (some on leadership) to clients. These courses can be delivered at a campus (e.g. Center for Creative Leadership in Greensboro, North Carolina, and other places), at a location in some major city (e.g. the American Management Association), at the client's location (e.g. Development Decisions International), or at some out-doors physically demanding setting (e.g. Pecos River Leadership Training). There are also thousands of very small firms across the country offering their training services to companies.[25]

To get a handle on the size of this training company component, consider only the largest of this variety, the American Management Association. The AMA offers professional development seminars (most 3-5 days), covering 24 distinct subject areas. The Leadership Area has 32 different classes. Interpersonal Skills, an area closely related to leadership, includes some 21 more. Thus the leadership dimension is not confined to just the term leadership and is hard to assess and count. Thirty percent of the AMA courses have a very strong leadership component. Seminars, webcasts, webinars, and online courses are offered throughout the year across 40 cities. I believe that the AMA teaches leadership to more students in the US than do all MBA programs combined. And the AMA is only one of a score of such large training companies.[26]

4. In-house Training Courses

The vast majority of companies in the US have some form of training normally within the Human Resource Management function. This training ranges from an orientation program in small companies, to extensive skill related courses in others, to multiple levels of management training in larger corporations.

A disturbing recent report reveals a huge gap in what is offered. While the average age of leaders going through their first level leadership training is 42, the average age of supervisors is 33—thus the average new leader gets trained nine years after becoming a leader![27] One could argue persuasively that the first line supervisor is the hardest leadership job of any level and more in need of assistance than any other.

Many companies have management trainee programs for new college graduates. Larger corporations (like General Electric) have invested in some form of centrally located corporate college or institution to help develop managers.

It is estimated that corporate spending on training (including both in-sourced and outsourced and for all types of training, not just for management and leadership education) was $356 billion in 2015.[28] No doubt much of that sum goes to technical training, but there is still a huge amount of training in-house that can be considered management or leadership training.

In summary, there are a very large number of professors, consultants, and instructors on multiple platforms across the country teaching a lot of people about leadership. This total field of leadership training clearly is distinct, distributed, and robust.

How effective is the teaching?

Virtually everyone who has ever taught or attended a leadership class or workshop is familiar with the technique of ending the class on a high note and handing out critique forms predestined to make a fair class look great and an average teacher world class. We called them "smiley sheets." Typically, the sheets reflected a rating of the entertainment value of the class.

In colleges, classes are rated more often than not by their sign-up count. For instance, among the most popular leadership-related courses at Stanford, "Interpersonal Dynamics," (aka "the touchy-feely class") has been voted the most popular elective for 45 years.[29] Popularity can be judged by how many people sign up for a particular class at a given institution. In the case of the elite executive leadership courses, will aspiring CEO's from the US and abroad continue to pay increasing top dollar for attendance?

But popularity is not the same as effectiveness.

Most serious teachers of this leadership subject agree with Howard Prince: "If one seeks only to provide learners with knowledge *about* leadership, then teaching leadership is primarily a matter of teaching in the same way one would teach any other subject in the humanities and social and behavioral sciences. One would need mainly to focus on defining a domain of knowledge and then engage the students in thinking about the subject."[30] That is doable.

But does cognitive learning about leadership make one a better leader? Can it change behavior? Doubtful!

Top scholars in the field share my doubt. It is really the top scholars in business schools who establish the tone and template for writing about leadership. They set the table for others teaching leadership in consultancies, companies, and other teaching institutions. Hence let's see what the academics say. It is pretty damning:

- Barbara Kellerman of Harvard's JFK School of Government offers a scathing critique:

"I'm uneasy, incredibly so, about leadership in the twenty-first century and the gap between the teaching of leadership and the practice of leadership. Moreover, I'm downright queasy about what I call the "leadership industry" – my catchall term for the now countless leadership centers, institutes, programs, courses, seminars, workshops, experiences, trainers, books, blogs, articles, websites, webinars, videos, conferences, consultants, and coaches claiming to teach people – usually for money—how to lead...

We don't have much better an idea of how to grow good leaders, or of how to stop or at least slow bad leaders, than we did a hundred or even a thousand years ago; that the context is changing in ways leaders seem unwilling or unable fully to grasp ... notwithstanding the enormous sums of money and time that have been poured into trying to people how to lead, over its roughly forty-year history the leadership industry has not in any major, meaningful, measurable way improved the human condition."[31]

- MIT's Professor of Management John Van Maanen notes:

"Even today, three-plus decades in, there's no real definition of [leadership]... We can make people more conscious of ethical dilemmas in business, of the difficulty of directing people in times of adversity, and the confidence and communication skills necessary to do so. But the idea that such skills can be transmitted so that you can lead anybody at any time, that's ideologically vacuous."[32]

- Stanford professor Jeffrey Pfeffer is an avid critic of the state of leadership study and teaching. The title of his book provides a giant clue to his perspective: *Leadership BS: Fixing Workplaces and Careers One Truth at a Time.* His summation: "The enormous resources invested in leadership development both in universities and in corporations have produced few results."[33]

And from another book by Pfeffer and Sutton: "...no book, consultant, class, or series of classes, including an MBA, can teach anyone how to lead even a small team, let alone a big organization. It is a craft you can learn only through experience. This lesson about leadership is evident throughout history, and remains true despite all the training and business knowledge that has been amassed."[34]

- Two Harvard Business School Professors, one now the Dean, severely decried the current state of leadership research and focus in academia:

"…research on leadership is at best at the periphery rather than the center of most schools that profess to educate the leaders of the future… there are few papers on leadership published in the most prominent academic journals; and there are virtually no doctoral courses on leadership…How can we explain this disconnect between the mission and everyday practice? Perhaps it is because leadership is an elusive construct, riddled with so much ambiguity that it is hard to define, let alone study systematically. Perhaps it is because it is hard to get tenure pursuing research on such a difficult topic. Perhaps it is because it is hard to grasp leadership unless you have been a leader. Whatever the reason, research on leadership has languished in the academy.

It is easy to enumerate the flaws of this genre of leadership literature: It seldom conforms to the norms of the scientific method; it employs casual and sometimes self-serving empirical evidence; it is rarely grounded in any well-established theoretical tradition. In short, it lacks intellectual rigor. However, in the absence of a credible alternate body of leadership research that is conducted with greater rigor while still being relevant and useful to practice, academics should not complain. We have what we deserve."[35]

- Author and college speaker William Deresiewicz argues that we seem to be producing leaders but don't have a clue what that means:

"There seem to be two possibilities. The first is that it means nothing at all, or whatever definition is useful at any given time. The second is that it simply means being in charge."[36]

- Professor and Director of Leadership at Australia's Monash Business School, Anne Lytle concurs:

"I think the vast majority of business schools do a completely insufficient job at developing transformational leaders."[37]

- Harvard professors Srikant Datar, David Garvin and Patrick Cullen sum it up:

"Virtually all of the top business schools aspire to 'develop leaders,' yet their efforts in this area are widely viewed as falling short".[38]

Get the drift?

To be fair, some classes in *academia* are well presented and useful, but the curricula are dominated by management topics and include only a smattering of leadership. Moreover, much of what leadership is taught is narrowly aimed at top leaders (CEO-COO). The professors are writing and teaching about the CEO's they know. And few are talking about the supervisor who has trouble getting people to show up on time.

Turning from academia to *consulting companies*, these firms feed on what is taught at the business schools. Hence their approach to leadership mirrors the mediocre results of the universities. Moreover, for most of these consulting companies, "leadership" is ancillary to their core area of expertise. Well-regarded firms like McKinsey, Bain and Boston Consulting Group are great at assistance in areas like strategy, mergers/acquisitions, or enterprise-wide transformation. But they have neither the expertise nor the desire to launch effectively into leadership development either for an executive or for an entire company. I believe few consulting firms are good at, or respected for, leadership development capability. With acknowledged bias, I believe my former firm, The Senn-Delaney Leadership Consulting Group, is one of few happy exceptions. Of their many clients I personally worked for, I would rank McDonald's Corporation as the most successful engagement.

Like consulting companies, the *training companies* also draw on what has been published. So, they fall into the same trap as the universities and most consulting companies. These training companies almost exclusively are production oriented with set classes given from off-the-shelf programs. These classes are rarely tailored for a given client. The vast majority of this training is offered by registration which means people elect, or are selected, to attend. Hence, these programs are most often not taught to intact work teams. Whenever you have a class "off-site with strangers" some insight may occur, but it is out of context.

Real and sustained leadership development has to occur in a setting with teammates and must relate to the business issues of the day. Unless the course or workshop is related to real work and real situations, it is just an academic exercise.

Finally, the *in-house training courses* are similar to the above training companies. Most trainers draw material from the above three other sources and therefore mirror their output. The scope, content, and value are all over the map, just like the companies. However, these in-house courses do have the benefit of having business relevancy, visible proximity, and bottom line scrutiny. If they were not perceived as valuable, they would be scrapped.

In sum, *academia, management consulting companies, training companies,* and *in-house training courses* all offer much of value, but none strikes at the heart of leadership.

I don't claim to have the total answer to what has been presented as a widespread and conflicting problem, but I believe I can add to the solution. Allow me in the next chapter to offer an alternative approach.

Chapter 3

A Totally Different Approach

**"Teaching leadership is complex;
therefore how it is taught has to be creative."**
Lata Dhir[1]

The approach to leadership I am proposing is a fairly radical change to what one sees in the current classroom both in substance and in style of teaching. My approach doesn't negate what is currently going on in universities and other leadership classes across the country. But it does add a new (and crucial!) dimension.

The idea came to me from my old boss General H. Norman Schwarzkopf. I had worked for "Stormin' Norman" in the Pentagon in the early '80's. After his retirement, I attended a speech he gave in 2001 on the topic of leadership.

**H. Norman Schwarzkopf, Jr.
General, US Army**

One quotation stuck:

> **"Leadership is both character and competency,**
> **and if I had to choose one, I'd choose character."**

Character over competency? Really? The implications for this statement are profound. I started thinking: How do you define each of these terms? Can they be taught? Can they be developed?

I started exploring this idea in my leadership classes and workshops. My teaching technique also served to get total audience involvement and to personalize the idea of leadership with each student.[2] From my perch in front of the class:

"I want to ask you to take several minutes to think about the best leader you ever personally knew. It could be anyone—the only requirement is that you know or knew the leader personally. Take some time and write down the name and position."

After a few minutes I asked for responses and got a wide range of answers including my father, a former boss, my English teacher, my scout leader, a high school wrestling coach, my first supervisor, a colleague, my grandmother, a neighbor, my battalion commander, a minister, and the current CEO of my company.

A Chinese manager offered, "Mao Tse-tung."

"Did you really know Chairman Mao?"

"I saw him once in a large public gathering."

"Please choose someone you knew personally. And everyone please now take a few minutes to write down a word or phrase that expresses why you picked this person." In essence I was asking, "What was *the leader's legacy?*"

As the answers came, I wrote down them down on two flipcharts attempting to divide them into two groupings, one for character and one for competency. Check marks indicated a second vote. This was the result:

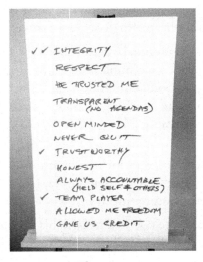

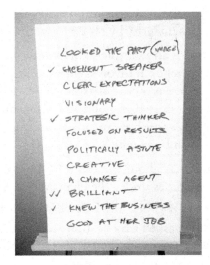

Character   *Competency*

I then spent some time allowing the class to discuss on which side I had very quickly placed their responses.

"Do you see the distinction between the two sides?"

Heads nodded.

Here is the basic model I offer:

	Character **(Who you are)**	**Competency** **(What you know/do)**
Definition	Principles Values	Skills, Knowledge Behaviors
Examples	Respect, Honesty Teamwork, Trust Accountability Integrity	Strategic Planning Communication Delegating Creating a vision

One student observed, "In general, competencies can be observed. They are actions, skills, behaviors. But character traits are internal and only implied by behaviors or actions. You can't see honesty or integrity, only its results."

"I concur. And it is important to underscore that we infer a character trait such as integrity by observing actions that indicate a high degree of this trait.

"Here is an example to help draw a clear distinction between character and competency. It involves communication: Good communication is universally accepted as a crucial aspect of leadership. Good communicating skills can be manifested in good listening, one-on-one coaching, public speaking, writing, and how to run a meeting, for example. These are all observable and can be taught."

But what about the desire to be open, candid, and inclusive with others? This comes under the character column. Decidedly different, yes, but this character trait, openness, is critical to good communication.

"When asked why he didn't communicate some very bad news to his people, a leader once answered, 'I don't know how.' Truthfully, he was afraid. He knew how to assemble the team and how to organize a talk. He was articulate and could express himself well in front of a group. Those were competencies. But he lacked courage. Moral courage is a very important character trait, and it is not a competency. The same for openness."

Another student asked, "What about a leader being a change agent? I know that is important. How does that fit in?"

I responded that John Kotter wrote two landmark books on change: The first was a very logical and compelling template for leading change, titled *Leading Change.*[3] In this book, the author lays out the competencies a leader needs for large scale organizational change. Knowing what to change, when, and how are all complex issues. And they are all skills or competencies. The second book, *The Heart of Change: Real-Life Stories of How People Change Their Organizations,* focuses on the emotional aspects necessary for effectiveness.[4] The second appeals more to the human elements a leader must display to motivate people to do something they are reluctant to do.

I explained that when it comes down to determining whether you are or are not going to be a change agent, it comes down to the character side of the above dichotomy. Are you open to change, open to recommendations for change, open to exploring, open to not knowing, open to taking a risk? These I argued are character traits and cannot be easily taught. But they are critically important.

A student asked, "How does an inspirational leader fit into this duality concept?"

"I believe Warren Bennis captured in a nutshell the inspirational aspect of a leader's character with this famous quote, 'A leader does not just communicate the change, a leader is the change.'[5] The speeches a leader uses, the words a leader chooses, the passion a leader shows, and the actions a leader takes are all behaviors that emanate from an inner personality, a sense of self identity, and core personal beliefs. I would answer you that inspirational fits on the character side."

I gave the students another example from the field of education: a story of two young women, Sue and Pat. In high school, the two were very similar and good friends. Sue was judged to be extremely bright, but not overly dedicated to studying. Pat was thought to be average in intelligence, but pursued her studies with a passion. Fast forward. The results were striking. "Perhaps you suspected," I said. "Sue did not finish college, and Pat, the hard worker, earned a Ph.D. I know you know of similar cases where a core attitude within a person's character made all the difference in outcome of a particular challenge or even of a life."

This topic of "grit being more important than brains" has been studied extensively. Stanford Psychologist Carol Dweck wrote: "There is no relation between students' abilities or intelligence and the development of master-oriented qualities. Some of the very brightest students avoid challenges, dislike effort, and wilt in the face of difficulty. And some of the less bright students are real go-getters, thriving on challenge, persisting intensely when things get difficult, and accomplishing more than you expected."[6] Author Angela Duckworth gives this concept color with her *New York Times* best seller *Grit: The Power of Passion and Perseverence*.[7] Grit is a character trait. Important? Yes.

I offer you the reader another example from military history. Early in his career, George S. Patton participated in an early tank battle in World War I. In 1920 at Fort Meade, Maryland, he studied and experimented with tanks with his neighbor, Major Dwight D. Eisenhower. He studied military history extensively and supposedly even read German General Erwin Rommel's book. As a Lieutenant General slashing across France in 1944, Patton was unstoppable. Was he competent? Top notch. No one knew better than he how to maximize the use of armor, infantry, artillery, and air power. But his major attribute was a daring, unrelenting, audacious, desire for victory against his enemy. Bold: that is Patton's character. Important? I think so.[8]

And it is not as if character has never been thought of as an important aspect of leadership. "Plato asserted that the character of leaders makes a large difference in whether or not they are able to rule effectively on behalf of the community."[9]

According to Rachel Sturm, "There is a quite clear recognition in the current scholarly literature that leadership character is important but it is totally overshadowed by leader competency."[10] It is a mystery to me why this has been so. My reading suggests that the academic interest in "management" is about a century old, in "leadership" about half a century old, and in the "character" dimension of leadership, very recent.

What's the problem? Some find the notion of character to be too moralistic. Others may find that while character may be nice to have, it is not essential for effective leadership. Pfeffer and Sutton make a good case for this.[11] I suspect that it comes down to the difficulty of defining, measuring, and improving character, which happens to be the essential thrust of this book.

My fundamental argument is that character is very important for good leadership. It goes back to my basic definition of leadership:

> A leader   influences   a person or persons   to do something.

Thinking logically, if you don't have a **leader**, or if you don't have **followers**, or if you don't **do something**, leadership cannot exist. Pretty simple.

What is most compelling and intriguing then is the verb to **influence**.

How does character impact influence?

Character traits like integrity, openness, grit, integrity, respect, and accountability all build trust with the team you are leading, and trust allows you to have influence with that team.

> Character → Trust → Influence

I am not using character in the moral sense of righteous conduct. Many religions promote *honesty* in order for a member of the congregation to be a better person. The only reason I include *honesty* in my examples is because it makes a person more trustworthy to the followers. Similarly, the edict of *loving your neighbor* would not make my taxonomy, but *respect for others* would.

Now what about the question of whether character or competency is more important? I believe I could mount a good argument that neither one is more important than the other. If you have worked for incompetent leaders, you can personally relate to this. And if you have worked for leaders of poor character, you can painfully relate.

Whom would I choose? An Infantry company commander who allows his soldiers to commit war crimes (character flaw), or one who has no idea how to bring in effective artillery and air power to support his troops in combat (incompetent)?

For the civilian equivalent of this Hobbesian choice, whom would you choose? The executive who doctors the books to show more profits for a huge personal bonus (character flaw), or the one who repeatedly makes very poor business decisions resulting in bankruptcy and wholesale layoffs (incompetent)?

Clearly, good leaders have to be strong in **both** character and competency. I hope you aspire to be strong in both.

Think back on your own schooling, development, and training. With regard to the leadership imperative to communicate well, you may have taken courses on coaching, writing, or public speaking. You may have read examples of good and bad communication by leaders. You may have gained an intellectual appreciation for the importance of communication as a leader. I am sure they were helpful.

But show me the course that made you more open, candid, and inclusive with others. Pray tell, show me the course that moves the needle at all for you or any other student on this character trait of "openness."

And confounding it, openness is two-way: openness to keeping others apprised of what you know, and openness to accepting ideas from others to include feedback for you. All of this is character. It is not a competency—and rarely if ever is it taught.

The typical school or training program consists of a fairly good dose of leadership skills and competencies but is lacking in leadership character development. Here is an excerpt from a keynote speaker at an MBA convocation of a business school: "When we think about leadership, we focus too much on what leaders do… and we don't spend enough time on who leaders are—the character of leaders." Surprisingly it came from the Head of McKinsey's Global Consulting Practice.[12] I would wager a goodly sum that McKinsey's sizable consulting revenue stream has nary a penny coming from how the firm develops character in their clients.

Finally, to repeat, competency and character are both important. And because I firmly believe that leadership competencies are at least adequately covered in leadership texts, literature, and instruction, I will not spend much time in the rest of the book on the competency aspect of leaders or on how to develop competency in leaders. My focus from this point on is on the *character element of leadership*. And I trust you are now persuaded that character is very important for good leadership.

Perhaps you are wondering how one impacts character, or whether or not it is even possible to do so. There is a school of thought that holds that character is immutable from childhood. Some even say we are genetically predisposed. You either have it or you don't.

I disagree.

Later in the book, I will address the broad topic of character development, namely how to enhance, promote, and influence your character with some very specific recommendations for going forward.

But first, let us examine the concept of character itself. As we do that, I invite you to examine in depth and then to define your own character—more precisely, to examine and define the character traits you would most want to be known for.

It is up to you, after all, to define your leader legacy.

Chapter 4

What Is Your Leadership Character?

**"Definition of Character: From the Greek χαρακτήρ, ῆρος, ὁ.
An engraving stamp used on a coin to authenticate its worth;
later to mean the real inner value of a person."[1]**

I am almost positive you have had at least one job interview. You may also have been an interviewer. Then you know that recruiting searches and job postings often list character traits as crucially important. But while a lot of folks talk about character being important, its description is typically amorphous and ill-defined. A common refrain in recruiting is that character is important, but with no specificity:

- Managing Director of a Global Trading Company,

   "When we hire people, we always hire for attitude. We don't hire for skills."[2]

- TV anchor and C.E.O. NY City Production Company,

   "You hire for character and teach people skills."[3]

- Florida small town Police Chief,

   "We hire someone for attitude, 100 percent. We can train you for everything else – all the skills it takes to be a police officer."[4]

- Investor writ large, Warren Buffet,

   "In looking for people to hire, you look for three qualities: integrity, intelligence, and energy. And if they don't have the first, the other two will kill you."[5]

But I know of many hiring managers who later wished they'd had a better handle on the character of a job candidate, before the offer was made. Character is very hard to discern from a resume and very tough to assess in one interview or even several. Assessment often comes from a gut feeling when the candidate is asked about overcoming obstacles in the past, or from generalities shared confidentially from a candidate's references.

Retiring from the army, I proudly listed "integrity" on my resume as a character strength, having had it favorably commented on in my personnel dossier. One recruiter told me to take it out. Why? It could be that the position required "going along with the good ol' boys" more than being a staunch supporter of legalities, truth, and transparency. Perhaps, but this view I believe to be an anomaly. Most managers at any level want a new hire to have solid integrity, even if they can't define it. And most cannot.

While it is certainly okay to say someone has excellent character, it is also quite imprecise.

Let's examine the various meanings and shades of "character" before asking you to draft your own.

Sometimes character can have a decidedly moral theme. When a particular type of behavior, often termed "sexual misconduct," is exposed, that person's character comes into question. News media routinely publicize stories where a general, executive, politician, or other high-profile person had an affair, or worse. This is often cited as a character problem.

On one occasion, I personally had to deal with a senior executive who had an affair with, and then began harassing, a young female manager in the organization. The President and Chief Operating officer referred to it as a "zipper problem." Happily, it was resolved in favor of the woman with swift and tough action by the CEO, a man of character and the most decisive leader I have ever met.

While character includes matters of sex, fidelity, and respect, it is not so narrowly defined. Character is a much larger concept than sexual morality. It includes qualities of integrity, being a team player, accountability, openness, and a lot more.

David Brooks draws a distinction between two interpretations of the word character. Character can mean being a nice person (generosity, self-sacrifice) or it can mean being an effective leader (grit, tenacity, resilience, accountability).[6] Richard Reeves offers a similar message: "Character…is not synonymous with morality. Character combines qualities like drive and prudence that could—but might not—serve moral ends. It's much more prosaic, but it may be more important."[7]

As I have stated, I take the stance that character is essential for leadership, and I define it to include only those elements that breed trust and effectiveness, not those elements that fall under the umbrella of morality.

As a Lieutenant Colonel, I once convened what some termed a "come-to-Jesus meeting" with my officers because it was common knowledge that they were going after the ladies in a foreign land while their wives were at home. I made the argument that soldiers would not trust their leaders if they knew the officers would violate the trust of their wives. I was never sure that my exhortations were taken for more than just morality and religious preaching. But to me it was an issue of trust and integrity, critical to good leadership. Unknown until I left the unit, I had received the nick-name "The White Knight," which pleased me.

Another view of character needs clarification. Some authors portray character as simply something you have or do not have, while I take a much more nuanced stance.

Consider the concept of courage, which could include bravery in battle but also could include the moral courage to stand up for what is right, or speaking out for injustices in any walk of life. I believe it is fallacious to simply look at that concept and conclude that a person either has courage or does not. A much more accurate view is that each one of us has some measure of courage as opposed to having all or none. I also believe a character trait like courage can vary over a person's lifetime and in different scenarios.

To think of a character element in a binary, either/or manner is neither accurate nor helpful. Below are five character traits shown in a bi-polar fashion. The chart below portrays character traits as if you have it or you don't. When you make this incorrect assumption you do a disservice to the whole idea of character.

Polar opposites? Much too simplistic:

(+)	(-)
Honest in communications	Dishonest in communications
Accountable	Irresponsible
A team player	Self-serving
Brave	Cowardly
Respecting	Disrespecting
High integrity	No integrity

This is wrong. In reality, each of the sample character traits shown above is not an either/or choice, but has its own spectrum. When we stop and think about any of the above traits, we know there is a wide range for each variable. Most leaders are somewhere between the two end points. Most of you are between the two end points. As am I.

To return to a previous theme, "Are these character traits really important to effective leadership?" I say, not yes, but hell yes!

For example, take the first one from the table, Honesty in Communications. From my experience, this is sorely lacking in many (if not most) companies. It might not be outright lying, but people shade what they say by what they wish others to hear, or say one thing and do something else. According to one survey, only 17% of America's working adults agree or strongly agree with the statement that their organizational leaders say exactly what they mean.[8] Pretty pathetic.

"Walk the talk," is a plea heard often. Other admonitions:

- From Ralph Waldo Emerson,

  "What you do speaks so loudly, that I cannot hear what you say."

- From General George Patton:

  "Say what you mean and mean what you say."

- And on assignment in the heart of Texas, I heard this proverb:

  "Don't write a check with your mouth that your body can't cash."

And while these quotes are telling, they don't tell the accurate story. They lack precision. Where is any leader on this scale between Honest in Communications and Dishonest in Communications? Who knows? Any character trait under examination needs specificity to be meaningful. Add observable gradations 10-1, and voila, you have a scale:

Honesty in Communications

10. Painfully honest, unfiltered, holding nothing back, regardless of impact

9. Strong moral courage to bring up salient points, even if difficult

8. Willing to offer a contrary point of view

7. Often supports an unpopular point of view

6. Honest but often does not express it openly, or forcefully

5. Can be totally silent when input could help
4. Sometimes holds back key information in order to sway a decision
3. Abuses statistics or other tools to change the nature of the information
2. Lies, misleads, distorts facts
1. Lies habitually, a crook; should be in jail

Now you have access to a useful rating system. It would be quite easy for you to rate a colleague or yourself in "honesty in communications" on a scale from one to ten. This chart makes the point that there are degrees of honesty in communications. Considering these shades adds texture and realism. Likewise, there are shades of all other character traits. The chart also infers that a person can move up or down on the scale. For instance, if someone is judged to be a "six" on honesty in communications, movement up the scale could be a very worthwhile personal goal.

Another often misunderstood aspect of character is that it differs between professions and walks of life. Consider:

- "Patriotism" might be high on the list for a person in the military, but may not make the list of another.
- "Commitment to doing no harm" has a long legacy in the medical profession, but might not fit in others.
- "Respect for the law" has a place for policemen and jurists, but might not be at the top of another's list.
- "Empathy for poor or neglected" may be crucial for those engaged in social services, but not for others.

Unlike most other authors on this subject (and I have read a bunch.), I firmly believe that there is no one exclusive or universal list of character traits. Nor should there be. Certainly, there will be common themes and considerable overlap. But there should be variations for different careers, different people, different roles, and different times in our lives. Let me suggest one more example to make this point.

I don't see how a person could have the positive character trait of being an outstanding parent until the time comes. Certainly, we are moved in that direction by closely observing our parents over the years, and most of us aspire to be good parents. But the "big day" really makes that happen. I am not convinced that a person who doesn't have or doesn't desire to have a child can have in their character portfolio "being a good parent." I also believe one can improve in this very desirable character trait of being a good parent over a life time. As a father, I think I have.

I once argued in my class that "integrity" was so foundational it should top any list of character traits. A student responded that "openness" was more fundamental. "If a leader had a problem with integrity, but was absolutely closed to any form of feedback, the issue of integrity would never be addressed;" he argued. "But if the leader was open to feedback, even integrity could be improved." Case closed.

I now believe there is no single one, absolutely top-of-the-list trait for everyone.

And I would be hard pressed to place integrity or any other value over parenting for the new mom or dad described above.

Thus, it is my view that each person should choose and claim a unique set of character traits, and that no one particular trait needs to be number one for everyone. Unlike many of my colleagues who opine on this issue of character, I believe the character traits should be chosen by the individual leader, should be tailored and refined by that person, and should serve his or her needs. I am in good company:

> **"Everyone has the obligation to ponder well
> his own specific traits of character.
> He must also regulate them adequately and not wonder
> whether someone else's traits might suit him better.
> The more definitely his own a man's character is,
> the better it fits him."**
>
> *Cicero*[9]

Your character description could have a religious element (like obeying God's word) if that impacts your leadership, a familial element (parenting, for example) if you are focused on leadership at home, and a professional element (such as living up to a code) if you are in a profession.

Your character description should also contain those character elements you wish to own as a leader in the workplace (e.g. integrity, respect). The possibilities are endless.

And if the list is too large you will end up lacking focus. Therefore, I recommend you narrow your selection to a handful or so of those at the top of your list. For this to happen you will have to do some soul searching, some reflection, and generate some personal commitment, which comes next.

In summation of my tutorial so far, character traits:

- Are for effective leadership, not moral purposes.
- Are not binary; they have a range.
- Need to be described using observable behaviors.
- Differ based on the individual and his/her profession.
- No one set fits all, and no one trait should always top the list.

Let us now turn to how you can define your character.

There are a multitude of biographies written about great people and their character descriptions.

A shorter version would be to write a paper of a few pages, or even a paragraph on yourself. That is very hard to do. The paragraph or page approach is also hard to use to measure your character or to demonstrate improvement. I offer an approach and format that is relatively easy and provides the opportunity for measurement.

It is my belief that the simplest and most effective way to describe character is to do so with a list of character traits described in enough detail to make them real and meaningful. I suggest this is best done by first coming up with a list of one word traits and then providing some specifics and detail for each trait. From my experience, this format is easier to accomplish and fits well into the measurement and improvement discussions that will follow in the next chapter.

I will start with the list of traits. Later in the chapter we can address the specifics for each trait.

Your task is to come up with a list of character traits you cherish and wish to live by. Each person doing this exercise will arrive at different traits. And each person will pick a particular trait because it has a unique meaning.

For example, "teamwork" could include your family, community, work group, or entire company, or larger. A profound question is, "What size team are you playing on?"

And I guarantee "integrity" has many meanings. Here is G.K. Chesterton's take on it:

**"Right is right even if nobody is doing it.
Wrong is wrong even if everybody is wrong about it."[10]**

35

One of the most bizarre discussions I have experienced on integrity was with a team of executives I coached. To them it meant, "Deliver on time." It started with the fact that the CEO had a propensity to be late for every meeting. If he said the meeting would start at 10, his people knew it would start any time between 10:15 and 10:30. It was a joke, but not a happy joke. This lack of punctuality spilled into a culture of missing deadlines and milestones. Trust was eroded; teamwork was nonexistent. To this team, if someone said she would do something by a certain date, it was always late. You could not count on anything or anybody. They vowed to change this. And it all started with the CEO arriving at the meeting at the time he said he would. Otherwise he would have not done what he promised to do. He would have lied.

Another example is "honesty," which can have many meanings and can vary greatly with context. Honesty could apply to discussions with colleagues, leveling with your family, financial affairs, submitting reports, or even being honest with yourself.

Note what Shakespeare said:

"No legacy is so rich as honesty."[11]

What did he know? I would argue that it is still unclear what the bard meant by honesty. Each character trait will require you to personalize it by putting some definition into each word, some specifics that make it a lot less nebulous. That will come later. For now, I suggest you simply come up with a short list of character traits you wish to emulate.

To assist you, I have included in the next few pages what I found in the literature on character traits. It is presented only for you to *scan* in order to pick out which appeal to you personally.

It is interesting to note that this intellectual search has been going on since (at least) 350 BC, when Aristotle proposed these 12 virtues in his work, "Nicomachean Ethics," named after either his son or father, both called Nicomachus:[12]

Courage	Good Temper
Temperance	Friendliness
Generosity	Truthfulness
Magnificence	Wit
Magnanimity	Justice
Right ambition	Practical Wisdom

Three professors from the Western University in London, Ontario, Canada, recently recast Aristotle's 12 virtues into 11 "leadership character dimensions":[13]

Judgment	Integrity
Transcendence	Temperance
Drive	Justice
Collaboration	Accountability
Humanity	Courage
Humility	

An Oxford scholar has proposed these four "cornerstones of character":[14]

Integrity	Accountability
Humility	Courage

Ronald E. Riggio of the Kravis Leadership Institute, Claremont McKenna College has created a Leadership Virtues Questionnaire with four cardinal virtues:[15]

Prudence	Temperance
Fortitude	Justice

Three principals from a company called "Leadership Worth Following" created a "Worthy Model" with nine dimensions:[16]

Personal Integrity	Power
Ethics	Humility
Openness	Gratitude
Courage	Forgiveness
Organizational Integrity	

One author, focusing on character development of children in schools, again makes a distinction between *moral* and *performance* character. In *moral* character, he includes such items as kindness and humility. In *performance* character, he lists the following:[17]

Industriousness	Drive
Prudence	Determination
Ability To Defer Gratification	

A firm called VIA (Values in Action) founded by professors from the University of Michigan has come up with 24 "character strengths" under six broad "virtue categories":[18]

Wisdom and Knowledge	**Justice**
Creativity	Teamwork
Curiosity	Fairness
Judgment	Leadership
Love of Learning	**Temperance**
Perspective	Forgiveness
Courage	Humility
Bravery	Prudence
Perseverance	Self-Regulation
Honesty	**Transcendence**
Zest	Appreciation of Beauty and Excellence
Humanity	Gratitude
Love	Hope
Kindness	Humor
Social Intelligence	Spirituality

A West Point father-son team came up with these "six habits of character":[19]

Courage	**Humility**
Integrity	Selflessness
Duty	Positivity

Now please take some time to *scan* all of these charts and choose those most important to you.

My recommendation is to pick five to eight traits that fit the way you aspire to lead. It has been attributed to George A. Miller that there is magic in the number seven, plus or minus two. He maintains that this is a pattern governing the process of our mind. I subscribe to his theory because it seems to fit my mental process. A shorter list is less meaningful. A longer list gets cluttered. However, neither the number nor the wording is etched in stone—you can also modify it later.

Do it fairly quickly, but buy into it. It should be yours, nobody else's.

...I assume you have accomplished this first step of defining your desired character. Good job! You have set yourself apart from most people—something that leaders tend to do.

To finish the second step, I am introducing a new, supporting concept.

In order to nail down the meaning of terms, I recommend that each character trait be amplified by "guiding behaviors." These are example behaviors that indicate the presence of the character trait. They should be "guiding" you in your journey to improve a particular character trait. They are descriptive, not exhaustive. And because they are called "behaviors," they are observable. Very importantly, they can be seen or heard. This addition of guiding behaviors adds specificity and context to the character trait.

Here is an example of one person's guiding behaviors for integrity:

Guiding Behaviors for Integrity
• Shows consistency between words and actions
• Honors and fulfills all commitments
• Confronts prejudice and corrects intolerant behavior
• Has no tolerance for dishonest behavior
• Role-models the highest standards of behavior
• Adheres to ethical standards in dealing with all stakeholders

Again, note the one-word character trait *integrity* is hard to see, define, and even explain clearly. But the guiding behaviors provide definition, specificity, and clarity by describing what can be observed. In other words, the trait *integrity* is implied by an observation of the guiding behaviors. And again, there are five to eight guiding behaviors, for simplicity.

This example is from an executive I coached. It worked for him. Yours needs to be tailored to you and your life.

Your task now is to craft the guiding behaviors for each of the character traits you selected. This should again take some considerable introspection and reflection.

I believe that the format on the next page will be most useful for you. I am a stickler for brevity and simplicity, so please use this format and limit it to one page.

Note there is room for one word or phrase for each trait in the first column (e.g. Integrity) and more room for the observable guiding behaviors for each trait in the second column. For the guiding behaviors, use the same grammatical construction as shown before, with an action verb for each guiding behavior. (e.g. Confronts prejudice and corrects intolerant behavior.) Finally, leave open the final column on the right for grading.

I am pretty prescriptive about this method (my best friends would say obsessive) because this format will serve you well later for surveys, feedback, and quantification.

This is the place in this book where you have to do some work before you read on. It will take a bit of time. Consider it a first draft. You can refine it later.

Once completed, you have now created your own personal Desired Character Profile. This is a huge step. Good job! And shame on you if you are just reading this and not doing it. It can be a highly insightful exercise.

You now have defined for yourself your own desired leadership character. And to reiterate, this was not an exercise to see how you can be a more moral and kind human being. It was an exercise to see how you can improve your leadership character so that people will trust you more and be more inclined to follow you as their leader.

Your Desired Character Profile is a description of what kind of leader you aspire to be. When you move to another job, company, community, or life, you will be remembered with this spotlight on your leadership. This will be your leadership legacy.

Now to the next chapter, which describes how to measure and then improve your leadership character.

"A man's character is his fate."

Heraclitus[20]

	Desired Character Profile	
Character Trait	**Guiding Behavior**	**Rating (1 - 10)**
A. _____		
	1.	
	2.	
	3.	
	4.	
	5.	
	6.	
B. _____		
	1.	
	2.	
	3.	
	4.	
	5.	
	6.	
C. _____		
	1.	
	2.	
	3.	
	4.	
	5.	
	6.	
D. _____		
	1.	
	2.	
	3.	
	4.	
	5.	
	6.	
E. _____		
	1.	
	2.	
	3.	
	4.	
	5.	
	6.	
F. _____		
	1.	
	2.	
	3.	
	4.	
	5.	
	6.	

Chapter 5

How Do You Improve Your Leadership Character?

**"You cannot dream yourself into a character;
you must hammer and forge yourself one."**

James A. Froude[1]

You have just completed an important task. Using a verbal template, the *Desired Character Profile*, you have defined the character you aspire to be. This is extremely important. And you are much farther ahead than most on the journey to improving your leadership. Now comes the key question, which is the title of this chapter. How do you improve your leadership character?

In broad terms it will entail getting feedback and engaging others in dialogue, then committing to improve, then making small positive steps which will become habits that strengthen your leadership character.

Before getting to very specific steps that I recommend, I want to give you a brief look at the research and scholarship in this field of "leadership development." This will provide you with a broad understanding of what the social scientists have to say about this field and what principles should be applied in its pursuit.

In the field of psychology, there is a broad area of study of the personality, typically defined as "relatively enduring patterns of behavior that make someone unique and predictable." The notion of personality development has been studied extensively. Suffice it to say that our personalities develop over time and are influenced by a lot of factors. A widely used personality assessment instrument called the OCEAN Model provides a benchmark for personalities and plenty of data for research.[2] It is well accepted that dimensions from this test correlate highly with leadership effectiveness.[3]

One would think that leadership development as a subset of personality development would be well understood.

But how leadership is actually developed is reputed by many scholars to be shallow in research. Two experts in this field, Robert Kegan and Lisa Lahey, believe the focus in academia has been too much on the first word (leader) and what the leader does (leadership), and precious little on the second word (development), how a leader develops.[4]

A University of Washington professor, Bruce Aviolo, laments: "Unfortunately, one of the least researched areas in the science of leadership is in fact the science of leadership development."[5] He goes on to say, "Our search of the literature convinced me that the science of leadership development was at best in its infancy, since it represented an extremely small percentage of the work that had been done on leadership."[6] (And if, as some scholars describe, "leadership development" is in its infancy in the academic research world, I submit that "leadership character development" is only a twinkle in some father's eye, maybe mine.)

Even with this criticism of the research in the field of leadership development, there is strong agreement that leader development occurs over a long period of time. It is not one class, course, or book. It is not one assignment. It isn't one great boss or mentor. All of these help. Leadership development requires a measured blend of challenging assignments, good coaches who are also role models, and rich feedback that allows for maximum learning and integration with other experiences. And there are multiple opportunities for schooling at various levels of responsibility.[7]

The Center for Creative Leadership's Cynthia McCauley and Christina Douglas describe in detail how mentors can really help in leadership development.[8] In my study of Dwight D. Eisenhower's leadership development well before he made general, I found he was lucky to have three superlative bosses, Douglas MacArthur (a brilliant, egotistical strategist), George Marshall (an organizational genius), and Fox Conner (a renaissance man well versed in philosophy, history, and literature). All three were role models and coaches for the younger Ike. Conner was a true mentor.[9]

For developing your own leadership, your current level of education, experience, salary, or authority matters little. As a leader-in-training, you should search out strong role models, coaches, and mentors. You should strive to go to the best classes available, and you should seek jobs that provide a challenge and opportunity to grow. Your opportunity is to learn from both your successes and failures, and you should eagerly seek feedback from all sources.

But allow me now to narrow our focus even more from the area of leadership development to that of **leadership character development**, reminding you that the character component of leadership is my personal passion and the focus of this book.

There are three broad schools of thought on how character is developed:

1. Character is at least somewhat predetermined by genetics. Sounds absurd? Consider that a mother's desire to take care of her offspring is deeply instinctive just like a dog, cat, bird, or bear. One could argue that a woman has a genetic predisposition to parent well and that this instinct is later refined during her lifetime by her own mother and others. There is also some data to suggest some aspects of cultural values can be passed between generations. One social psychologist and Professor of Ethical Leadership at New York University's Stern School of Business, John Haidt, asserts that certain elements of character (or morality) are fixed in our genetic code.[10]

2. Character is formed after birth but before the beginning of adulthood. Some argue it largely happens by the early teens, others by the late teens. These formative years involve a lot of parent, community, and school socialization and mold the character a person manifests for the rest of his or her life. My management professor at Harvard, Jay Lorsch, believes that character is fully ingrained by the time a person reaches adulthood, having been shaped and honed over time by a lot of factors: family, community, schools, and experiences.[11]

3. Character is a life-long building process. Many well respected developmental psychologists argue that personality and moral development occur throughout one's life span. There is strong data to suggest that mental and character development do not peak at about age twenty-six like physical ability, but continue late in life.[12] Still other psychologists specializing in personality maturation hold that our values and morals are shaped at an early age, but can be modified and honed over a life-time.[13]

I subscribe to the last as my operative theory. Character builds over a lifetime.

Said differently by experts at the Center for Creative Leadership, "No doubt, leadership capacity has its roots partly in genetics, partly in early childhood development, and partly in adult experience....adults can develop the important capacities that facilitate their effectiveness in leadership roles and processes. People can use their existing strengths and talents to grow in their weaker areas and can significantly enhance their overall effectiveness through leader development work."[14]

This view is shared by Harvard's Harry Levinson: "Middle age is the vast gulf between 35 and the time when every man comes to terms with his own fate. It's the time of the greatest expansion of the human personality, when the mature adult is in the widest possible contact with his environment. But it is also a time when several things happen. He's psychologically aging, and realizes he's no longer as competent and powerful physically as he used to be. As this stage of life comes along, they [executives] increasingly must give up on the individual competition. They invest themselves in the development of other people and … with evolving a new sense of purpose about living."[15]

I conclude that the initial character of a leader is formed before adulthood but that a leader's character can be modified after that. This is not a trivial assertion. Otherwise, character development as an adult would be impossible, and this journey I am proposing for you would be meaningless. Probably your commitment to continue with this book and this process will be determined by the strength of your belief in whether or not leadership character can be developed in adulthood. I am going to present one more example of character development in an adult to try to seal my case and to steel your conviction. It has to do with the character value "patriotism."

In 1906, the Broadway genius, George M. Cohan (*Yankee Doodle Dandy*), sat down next to a Union Civil War veteran and asked what he had on his lap. The old soldier (my guess: in his 60's) looked down on a tattered Civil War flag (my guess: with 34 stars) and responded proudly, "It's a grand old rag." Cohan was inspired to use that exact quote in his great new song about the flag, then sporting 45 stars. After several weeks the song morphed to "A Grand Old Flag." Before then and since, the flag has been our fundamental national symbol for loyalty and love of country. It is a symbol of patriotism, a character value.

Now, take today's eighteen-year-old marine recruit who at best has only a modest dose of patriotism, which he got from parents, schools, and upbringing. Train and reinforce within this young person, over a four-year stint literally in view of the base's American flag, that the stars and stripes are to be revered as a symbol of our country. Require the marine to salute the stars and stripes as it passes in review or is hoisted up a flag pole. Bond this marine with buddies through tough experiences, difficult and distant, most of the time in our country's uniform and with the flag in view. Add emotion-charged music like the National Anthem or bugle calls. Show the marine the Iwo Jima statue with the flag being raised on Mount Suribachi. Cloak the caskets of best friends with our nation's flag and punctuate the ceremony with taps.

What will be developed without fail is a level of patriotism and pride in the flag that is emotionally off the charts and intellectually hard to fathom. I have seen it in the tears of a 90-year-old World War II veteran saluting the flag. I have felt it.

I see this as an example of the development over a period of time of one aspect of character, namely patriotism. Note you cannot just look at a person or talk with him and discern if he is patriotic. You can only observe the behaviors that are borne from patriotism. Patriotism is inferred. Also note it was a series of experiences the marine had over a period of time that shaped and developed patriotism.

Elements of character are discerned by observing behaviors that reveal the trait. Any character trait is developed over time by experiences. As you act in a certain way, good or bad, your character will be modified and solidified, and you will develop a slightly different view of a particular character trait. This is not a recent finding:

**"You become just by doing just acts;
you become brave by doing brave acts."**

Aristotle

Repetitive behavior becomes habit forming, and habits shape and mold character. Character development is akin to learning a new habit; it must be adopted, reinforced, and practiced in order to take hold.

Habits, like character traits, can be good or bad. One retail manager, for example, engaged over a long period of time in what could be called "white lies" with regard to his business reporting. This became a habit. And it began to feel okay to him, a natural way of operating. When the opportunity to "tell a whopper" occurred, his ethical gyroscope was numbed down to neutral, allowing him to make an egregious ethical error almost without thinking. If he had ever embodied the character trait of "honesty," he was no longer in touch with it. He had practiced his way out of it, one lie at a time.

Churchill said it like this:

"Character may be manifested in the great moments but it is made in the small ones."

Winston Churchill

The formation of character through small acts in the same direction over time will solidify the character trait for the large challenge that may come later in the job or in life. Far too many public figures who fall from grace in our society because of ethical or moral mishaps failed because their characters were not adequately cemented by habits earlier in their careers.

Now that we have covered the scope and nature of character development, allow me to offer to you three pieces of advice from having worked this issue for a number of years: The process has to be yours. You don't have to be perfect. And you must embrace feedback, as it is the essential ingredient in this character development process.

Own it. You not only have to own the character you aspire to be but you need to own the process for enhancing it. If you are going to put some time and effort into this process, make it worthwhile. To do that it must be personal. It has to mean a lot to you. Reflect. Look inside. It is called introspection. It can be difficult for some, but it is essential to properly assess, calibrate, and improve your leadership character. It will make you a better person. And, importantly, it will make you a better leader. It will add measurably to your legacy.

Don't fall into the trap of having to be perfect. Last time I checked there has only been one person without sin. Pursuing a good leadership character is a lot like trying to be a really good person—we all will come up short. None of us is perfect or ever will be. Perfection can be a trap! Be comfortable that this is a journey for improvement, as this admonition suggests.

Perfection	Excellence
Pressure	Flowing
Fear	Risk
Judgment	Accepting
Being right	Willing to be wrong
Doubt	Confidence
Destination	Journey

Welcome feedback. Notice I didn't say "be open to feedback." It is more than that. You really have to search it out from folks. And you have to receive it from them wholeheartedly, with applause and aplomb. That doesn't mean you have to accept it as gospel. But accept it as valid from their perspective. The way you accept feedback will determine the amount and quality of any feedback you seek in the future.

Feedback often has a negative tinge to it. We often think that feedback is for folks who need to improve, be fixed, or are in some kind of difficulty. That notion is foolish. If it helps you, any constructive feedback is positive, not negative. What olympic athlete does not have a coach for the purpose of getting honest feedback? High performers tend to be the hungriest for feedback. Football coaches spend more time coaching their stars than the second and third teams. As my buddy, former college football coach and scholar, Dennis Alimena says,

"Feedback is the breakfast of champions, not Wheaties."

Dennis Alimena

What follows is a short description of some feedback resources available. They are not part of the program I am recommending, which I will lay out shortly. I believe my approach is simpler, easier to use, and more effective. However, consider these as back-ups if you so choose.

The first instrument developed along these lines was a 1952 personality test called Myers Briggs Type Inventory. The MBTI gained wide acceptance over the years and has a huge international database. You may have experienced a derivative of this survey in a leadership or team building workshop, wherein participants using a self-administered questionnaire place themselves into one or more stereotypic leadership categories or styles. Later, the 360-degree feedback model came into use, providing perspective on a leader from boss, colleagues, subordinates and customers. The first is highly introspective; the second provides a wider view. Both provide fodder for reflection.[16]

There have been several attempts in the past few years to take the above survey approach and apply it to a person's character. A number of these are available on the internet and listed in the notes. Some offer constructive feedback for how to improve in a given area. Take them if you wish, but even the best of them will rate you based on some other set of character traits, not the ones you selected. Understandably, these firms offer their services for a fee. But my main critique of all these approaches is that they are not unique to you. They will only give you feedback based on your input onto a sheet of their character traits, not yours. In addition, they are self-rating instruments and not applicable to getting feedback from others.[17]

There are even some recent attempts to provide insight on character by playing games on line. These startup firms purport to shed light on how a candidate for a job might perform in a job based on how he or she performs in a game. Games range from solving mazes to managing a simulated sushi restaurant. Depending on results, the game developer can build a detailed analysis of a player's abilities and share them with an interested employer. An evaluation might tag a person as a potential leader for showing tenacity and grit, certainly elements of character. But again, not focused on the leadership character you personally aspire to become.[18]

Now to the program I recommend to improve your leadership character. It has four specific and relatively easy steps:

1. Rate yourself on your *Desired Character Profile* from Chapter 4. Be as honest as you can. Don't make the mistake of failing to see any room for improvement. This is good advice:

> **"The greatest of faults is to be conscious of none."**
>
> *Thomas Carlyle*

As you rate each guiding behavior, use a scale of 1 – 10, where ten means "excellent" and one means "needs considerable improvement." From my experience and based on normal tendencies, I predict your ratings will be fairly high. We tend to rate ourselves and others high on character issues, unless there is a severe problem. I have placed the scale 1–10 on the form to encourage you to not just resort to a max score, but to allow a very good score slightly lower than 10.

Following is what part of your one-page form might look like, with ratings ranging from 6 to 10 and averaging for integrity, 7.83. Note the example is to show the format and process I am recommending. Your personal *Desired Character Profile* will have your own character traits and guiding behaviors. And your ratings will obviously be different than this pro forma.

Desired Character Profile		
Character Trait	**Guiding Behaviors**	**Rating (1-10)**
Integrity	———	**7.83**
—	1. *Shows consistency between words and actions*	7
—	2. *Honors and fulfills all commitments*	8
—	3. *Confronts prejudice and corrects intolerant behavior*	6
—	4. *Has no tolerance for dishonest behavior*	9
—	5. *Role-models the highest standards of behavior*	10
—	6. *Adheres to ethical standards in dealing with all stakeholders*	7
Respect	———	
—	1. *Does not tolerate others' sexual or racist behavior*	9
—	2.	
—	3.	
—	4.	
	Et cetera	

2. Now enlist for feedback 5-10 people who know you fairly well. Consider your boss and spouse if you are so bold. Use your *Desired Character Profile* sheet. Keeping the process simple is crucial for success. Using a clean, one-pager makes it less onerous, and simple scoring with no requirement for verbal input makes it a quick and easy task. Allow them to mark the numbers in private and at their leisure.

Parenthetically, I believe you will build rapport and trust with these friends or colleagues with this action. I have seen this happen with my clients. When a senior manager sat down with colleagues and opened this door, it was amazing for me to observe the mutual trust grow and the rapport blossom between them.

But it can be an uncomfortable task for you to ask someone to rate your character. And it can be daunting for someone to do as you have requested. Unlike giving you feedback on your communication or planning skills, this can be perceived as rating your soul. Two suggestions to get around this hurdle, both used only **as a last resort** if this is a problem for you:

- Figure out a way to collect the responses anonymously. Not knowing the source of the feedback will limit its validity, but this may be necessary if you feel your colleagues will have great difficulty rating your character as honestly as possible. When this is done, you will have a good picture of which of the several character traits is your top strength and which is most in need of improving.

- Don't ask them to rate the whole list. Simply ask them to annotate your highest and lowest character trait, or of all the guiding behaviors, mark the highest and lowest. This will make it easier for them to fill it out and will make their assessment feel less critical.

3. I then suggest you have some one-on-one conversations with some or all of these colleagues. This will flesh out your understanding of what you are currently doing that is good and what you are currently doing that distracts from your intended character. This style is less confrontational. Strive for specific examples of behaviors. The openness and effectiveness of these conversations will be directly proportional to how much rapport you have with these folks and how open—no, *welcoming*—you are to feedback.

4. It is now up to you to decide what you wish to work on. Your commitment is critical. If you do not select a meaningful item or items to work on, not only will the process be in vain, it will no doubt alienate those who have invested in your process. You should inform those people of your commitment and enlist their assistance as you proceed.

My guess is that your slight changes in behavior indicating an improved character will seem to you to be easy to do and small. But they will seem to others to be positive, significant, and enormous.

Recapping your accomplishment: You have carefully defined the leadership character you wish to uphold and live. You have put enough specifics on it that it is both personal to you and actionable by you. You have measured it using numbers. You have received useful feedback as to where you are strong and where you can improve. You have committed to a course to enhance your leadership character.

You are now prepared to continue your life and work with the intention of replicating this process in six months or a year. You may wonder if you will have enough meat to work with, namely specific actions to take to demonstrate movement. I can assure you that you will. I can also predict that you will by necessity take small steps, one at a time.

> **"The leader never lies to himself,**
> **especially about himself,**
> **knows his flaws as well as his assets,**
> **and deals with them directly.**
> **You are your own raw material.**
> **When you know what you consist of**
> **and what you want to make of it,**
> **then you can invent yourself."**
>
> *Warren Bennis*[19]

Chapter 6

Helping Your People Become Great Leaders

"Leadership is not defined by the exercise of power but by the capacity to increase the sense of power among those led. The most essential work of the leader is to create more leaders."

Mary Parker Follett
A top scholar of her day, 1924[1]

Peter Beresford, CEO of McDonalds of the United Kingdom, was a brilliant marketer, a change agent, an eloquent spokesman for the organization. As his coach at the time, I quickly discovered that his greatest strength was in spotting, encouraging, and promoting outstanding leaders. Of his six or so vice presidents, a young Englishman by the name of Steve Easterbrook was his top guy.

Steve was then in charge of 150 McDonald's restaurants in the greater London area. Not only did Peter see superior sales and operations numbers from Steve's region, he perceived a man who could lead, who could see the bigger picture, and who was a masterful communicator. I recall Steve coaching his fellow Regional VP's. I even recall Steve coaching me as the consultant.

Fast forward, Steve was later promoted to CEO of McDonald's UK business; he then assumed the executive role for all of Europe. In 2015 he was promoted to CEO of the Chicago-based global McDonald's Corporation, serving 68 million customers daily in 36,615 outlets in 119 countries.[2]

I tell this story not because of Steve's obvious talent and meteoric rise, but to explain the pride and satisfaction of Peter Beresford. Peter is rightly proud of the leader he launched. By coaching, assisting, supporting, and encouraging Steve, Peter made Steve a better leader. In a real sense, Steve Easterbrook is Peter Beresford's leadership legacy.

The younger leaders we assist, cultivate, encourage, and develop will be with the organization long after we leave. This legacy I argue is more important than anything else we might have been able to accomplish—it beats increasing sales, orchestrating an acquisition, launching a new product line, upgrading some system, or streamlining a manufacturing operation.

It has been my observation and experience that people rarely get rewarded or acclaimed for their leadership efforts in developing leaders. I can recall a fellow battalion commander in Germany by the name of Billy Gavan bragging about his "stars," the young officers he was bringing along. He got no accolades for that. But is this mindset not at the core of leadership?

Think back on what leader helped develop you. In what way did he or she assist? And consider how much you are assisting in the development of leaders on your team. Want to improve in that arena? This is the essence of this chapter.

What follows are highlights (in my words) from the "Handbook of Leadership Development"[3] where this topic is wonderfully described by the Center for Creative Leadership's Cynthia McCauley and Ellen Van Velsor:

In developing the leadership of your charges, you can teach techniques and skills, provide opportunities for challenging assignments, reward the person monetarily, or via promotions, send to a course, and document in writing or orally what a great leader this person is.

Throughout America there are a host of schools and courses for developing all aspects of leadership competency. They range from a supervisor's course put on locally by the American Management Association to a course designed for CEO's like CCL's Leadership at the Peak or the Harvard Business School's Advanced Management Program.

Most scholars in this area agree that leadership development is a process that occurs largely outside the classroom. By varying the challenges and opportunities of a budding leader, you present a number of experiences that teach more than any course ever could. The leader will flourish if this occurs in a robust feedback environment.

Leadership development also is greatly enhanced by role models one can observe. We all copy the behavior of people we admire and are close to. It starts at birth. And it clearly continues throughout life.

One chapter in the handbook affirms that "no single developmental event, no matter how powerful, is enough to create lasting change in an individual's approach to the tasks of leadership. Leader development is a lifelong, ongoing process."[4]

But recall my assertion that there is a dearth of material, effective course work, or even discussion about leadership *character*. It gets minimized because of a widespread emphasis on leadership *competency*. Recall the example of George Patton: His leadership competency came from a life time of study, observation, and experience. In terms of competency, his was outstanding— but most will agree that what set him apart was his audacity. And that is character. (Like us all, he had his flaws, too.)

My focus on character and character development is borne of the conviction that this is how a leadership legacy is created. Your legacy will be created partly by the character you manifest and partly by how much you assisted others in this regard.

Probably this is your first question: "Whom should I assist in this area of leadership character development?"

I would wager that most readers already have pretty good competency and experience at assessing leadership. More than likely you have been working with your team and watching reactions and results over time. You have seen them in action. You have seen them with small or large successes and failures. You have measured their results. You have written appraisals. This assessment function is key both to help you pick the leaders you wish to assist and also to advise specific steps for the individual to take. Note that leadership assessment is not a recent discovery:

"No man is more valiant than Yessoutai. No one has rarer gifts.
But as the longest marches do not tire him,
as he feels neither hunger nor thirst,
he believes that his officers and soldiers
do not suffer such things.
That is why he is not fitted for high command."

Genghis Khan (of an assistant)[5]

But don't make the mistake of writing someone off too soon. It would make more sense to discern both what the person needs to work on and whether or not the person wants to do so.

Another caution: Don't fall into the trap of seeing people as either leaders or followers. You have heard the expression, "Lead, follow, or get the hell out of the way!" This is often quoted and has some merit in getting people to move. But it again places people in the role of either a leader or a follower. I maintain we are all leaders and followers. Sound outlandish?

Consider who in this country is not a follower in some dimension. Do you know anyone who does not work for, or report to, someone? The CEO of General Electric reports to a board. The small business owner is accountable to his customers. The Chief of Staff of the US Army reports to the Secretary of the Army. The President is responsible to the American people and can be impeached by the Congress. You can say the pope reports to God. When she was alive, I reported to my wife, without question.

And I believe there are precious few who are strictly followers. There are too many informal connections where people network with and greatly influence others. As outlandish as it sounds, some even lead their titular leaders. I am sure you have seen cases where a junior person persuaded his or her boss to do something the boss might not have been inclined to do. When you define the central function of leadership as "influence," few in any walk of life do not influence others.

And what CEO would not want a company of leaders? A company of leaders does not mean a bunch of people who will not follow orders, as in "too many chiefs, not enough Indians." A company of leaders is to have a hoard of people who are eager and willing to positively influence all aspect of the business. What's not to like? We want people to follow orders and instructions and not to challenge legitimate leaders; in that sense they are great followers. But there are numerous occasions where we hope followers will jump in, take the initiative, and influence others—which is to say, lead.

Even the experience of a plebe (freshman) at West Point is one of leadership. I remember my father saying that, as a plebe on the parade ground his first summer, he had envied a dog lying in the shade of a tree. Years later I had a similar sentiment thinking that I was lower than a junk yard dog.

But these first-year cadets are routinely called on to influence others in various roles, some official, some not. I was totally flabbergasted on one occasion seeing one of my roommates getting ready for gym class putting his athletic supporter on backwards. In my lifetime I cannot recall ever having seen a funnier sight! Our squad leader then laid down the law, "Do not come out to formation until your roommate is in proper uniform." Never did I suspect that I would be teaching a very smart 18-year-old how to put on a jock strap. This was leadership of a plebe by a plebe, both memorable and hysterical.

Then there is the notion that all of us are leaders and followers at the same time. Rensis Lickert coined the concept in his linking pin concept as shown below:[6]

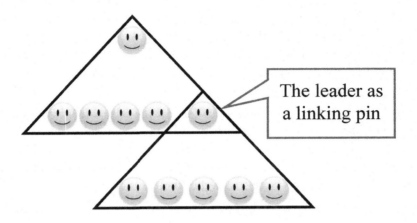

The leader as a linking pin

In a real sense the leader above is judged by how he or she operates in both groups. In the top, she is a follower and team player with peers. In the bottom, she is the leader. Lickert's idea is that the linking pin role is crucial. Simply stated, "Is the message discussed at the top carried to the bottom without noise and vice versa? Are the two triangles working in sync for maximum effectiveness or at odds with one another, resulting in frustration and inefficiency?"

Looking at the above chart, it seems to me that a leader can coach and develop anyone—up, down, or sideways. Coaching can occur at any level and in any direction. Although I recall vividly my wife telling me, "You have been gone all week consulting executives on how they can improve. I want you to leave it at the door!"

The real question is, "Do you have the rapport and personal connection to make it happen?" If you already have a mentoring relationship with someone in your group or elsewhere, you probably have mutual accord to proceed. If you have a good working relationship with a peer or even a boss, you likewise could proceed. But the typical relationship is between you and your subordinates, between manager and direct reports. This connection already has some history with coaching or at least end-of-year performance evaluation. I suggest you start there.

There is an advantage to approaching your whole team. No one will feel left out. I can recall one of the finest leaders I ever knew, Lieutenant Colonel Glynn Mallory, an Infantry Battalion Commander at Fort Carson, Colorado. On one occasion, Glynn had a fairly extensive coaching discussion with one of his officers. Later another young officer came up to Glynn and asked when he was going to be coached. Glynn responded with a degree of sarcasm, "Lieutenant, every time I am talking to you I am coaching you." Here was an outstanding coach. His people knew it and did not want to be left out. So taking on the whole team has some advantages.

Bringing in the whole team gets rid of the fear that any one is being singled out, either for good or for bad. Moreover, the character development approach, which was described in Chapter 5 for you as a leader and which will be replicated shortly for your team, is predicated on excellent and valid feedback from peers. So working with the whole team can make a lot of sense.

Alternatively, you may wish to start with one or two until you get your legs under you with the process. This will allow you to team up with the one or two people with whom you have the greatest rapport and trust, both essential for the process to be highly successful.

Regardless, I advise caution that this coaching process be construed in the most positive light. It should not be for your top or your bottom performers, nor should it be so perceived by anyone. There is a strong belief in corporate America (as well as the military) that if someone is being coached, he or she is being counseled for poor performance or a bad mistake. But professional sports coaches really spend more time with the first-string starters than the reserves. Coaching is for everyone.

So, your task is to determine whom to assist, the best approach, and timing. While you are pondering that and before I spell out my suggested steps, allow me to do a deep dive on the concept of coaching. I want to elaborate on coaching because it is essential for the process I am recommending and because it is typically done poorly, from my observation.

I was once taught several very valuable lessons about coaching.

While working for a consulting company, we went through a process of learning how to coach. Our first task was to pick a colleague to "practice coach." The idea was to really have a meaningful, two-way conversation, one coaching the other, and vice versa. I looked around and picked a woman with whom I had worked on several assignments. I asked Michele Johnson if I could partner with her. I told her I probably had some biases around issues of race and gender and thought she might be able to assist.

She answered with understated sarcasm, "Bob I'd be glad to, and I think there are some other things I can help you with."

My response: "No, no, no, I can only take so much!"

She is a great coach and a good friend to this day.

Lessons learned:

1. Rapport is essential. Period. Full stop.

2. Here is a tricky one: You don't simply gain rapport; you give it, and it comes back in kind.

3. Coaching works best when it is reciprocal, when both parties are open to feedback.

4. I personally can coach better if I can answer this question in the affirmative, "I want to provide the person with some feedback in order to assist her, not to show her how damned smart I am." The latter is called a "gotcha."

Now before you approach one of your people to offer coaching, think about setting the scene. Place and timing are important. It might work better in the other person's office, not yours. Or maybe over a beer. You decide.

But maximizing your rapport, as stated before, is necessary. You need to develop a level of rapport that will enable you to perform as a coach. Easier said than done. You have to bring your relationship with this person to a point of trust where you can be totally honest and helpful with each other. Maybe impossible, but the closer you get, the more productive. I emphasize this point because your discussions are going to be about character which is very personal.

Two more coaching examples from my past—one poor, one excellent.

Just the other day, I was riding with my bicycle club with about 15 riders. We were doing about 16 miles per hour, and a gap formed. Someone could not keep up. This resulted in about seven riders keeping up with the leader, a 200-yard gap, and then about eight other riders followed, with me at the end (the sweep).

Assuming the mantle of "assistant to the ride leader," I pedaled hard to catch up with the last rider in front of the gap. In my sweetest voice I said, "We are so far back, nobody could hear us when we shouted 'gap' or even when

I blew my whistle. The last person before the gap should call that forward to the ride leader. Otherwise the leader will be ignorant of the gap."

"I am breathing so hard trying to keep up," she said, "I can't call out anything. Plus my mirror got fogged up."

"Who else should do this?" I asked. "Want me to clean your mirror?"

The answer: "[Unprintable.]"

The result of this coaching: Nada.

What went wrong? First, I had had previous experience trying in vain to coach this person. So rapport was not there. Also, the fundamental problem was not failure to be observant to the rear, or to call alerts forward, skills fairly easy to teach. The fundamental problem was in trying to help this rider to adjust her perspective so that she would take personal accountability for this aspect of our riding. That shift is in attitude or character, is much more difficult to effect. Plus looking inside my attitude meter, I am convinced that I wanted more to tell her about the problem she was causing than to make a difference in her outlook.

My life lesson, addressed earlier in this chapter and still in progress: look inside before you coach. What is your agenda? If this coaching session is for you rather than the other person, abort. I wonder when I will really learn that!

But I must acknowledge that there are times where immediate feedback is necessary, regardless. I can think of a fairly small safety violation in a nuclear power plant where I was consulting. Immediate correction irrespective of rapport was required.

I wasn't always such a lousy coach. I can recall a coaching conversation that went extremely well. I felt this guy really trusted me, and I clearly trusted him. This was important because our backgrounds could have gotten in the way. He was a retired US Navy Admiral; I was a veteran of the Army, not the Navy. I had retired as a Colonel, not a General. Conceivably, either of these issues could have been an obstacle. He was also of a different race, which could have impacted our relationship ever so slightly. Not a problem.

I had a wonderful and memorable conversation with this man over a long cup of coffee. I had talked to each of his direct reports and had a good read on both his strengths and challenges. He was well liked and extremely open to feedback. I also took the opportunity for him to provide me feedback on how I was doing with him and with his team. The conversation was two-way, personal, and rich. I think I asked questions more than I made

62

pronouncements. At the end he whittled down the issues to two or three things he wanted to do to improve his leadership.

"I'll take that aboard," he said.

I had never heard that naval metaphor before, but I loved it. In his vernacular, he said he would "own" the changes. Touchdown!

Lessons again: rapport, clean and simple, is essential. I also learned something that for me is very powerful. If you want someone to trust you, you have to trust that person. And please notice a technique that helps: coach each other. It can demonstrate how to be open to feedback. It makes it more of a level playing field and enhances rapport. What kind of feedback is useful to you as the coach? Well, rather than only having a "method," it is more effective to coach an individual with your focus being on what is wanted and needed, on what works. "What do you need from me today?" "How can I support you with that goal?" "Was my previous recommendation helpful and useful since we last met?"

Now on to the specific protocol which I recommend you adopt. The meeting content should be known in advance. This means familiarity with the notion of what leadership character is and how important it is. It also entails an agreement to go into this discussion freely. You can't dive into something so personal without foreknowledge and acceptance.

1. **First meeting**

   Lead by example. Like the motto of the Infantry Leader, "Follow me!" Start by role modeling: Demonstrate that you have done what you are asking to be done. Show your *Desired Character Profile* discussed in Chapter 4.

   Share with this person what you know so far and where you are putting an effort.

   Ask for feedback on how you are doing.

   In addition to helping you personally with your character journey, the discussion will give your colleague an example of how to proceed.

   Let the person know your expectation that he or she is to follow suit.

2. **Second meeting**

   Ask the person to start his or her own *Desired Character Profile*.

   Walk the person through the process in Chapter 4 and have the person choose 5-7 character traits important to him/her.

Having done this yourself already and having discussed it with this person, yours may be okay. Or yours might be closely aligned with the values of your company or institution, in which case it might be appropriate for that person as well. Key is ownership. If your colleague cannot own it, let the person change it. Ownership is critical.

Once the person buys into a set of values they choose to aspire to, ask the person to draft the guiding behaviors for each trait as described in Chapter 4. Urge your person to use the format and verbal style, but come up with guiding behaviors that are appropriate. He or she should use words that are personally meaningful. This most likely will take some time and is proper for a homework assignment.

3. **Third meeting**

    Start with a review of what your person has worked on for traits and behaviors.

    Then ask the person to rate his or her own character on the profile sheet. It shouldn't take a long time but provide some privacy and quiet time to accomplish this. I estimate about 10 minutes.

    Then go over the rating form getting clarification around which issues are of special interest to your protégé. Thank the person for being honest.

    When appropriate, ask permission to provide feedback and do so. This could be in the form of you filling out the person's *Desired Character Profile*.

    Homework assignment before your next meeting: Ask the person to have similar discussions with 5-6 other colleagues/friends. The suggestions earlier in this chapter and in Chapter 5 with regard to how to approach people when you went through this process are quite valid here.

4. **Fourth meeting.**

    Ask your person to let you know what was learned.

    Then ask the person to articulate what area they intend to work on. Try for one or two. A laundry list will overwhelm anyone.

    Thank your protégé for the openness and trust.

    Commit to discuss progress in six or twelve months.

In concluding these instructions and this discourse on helping a colleague become a better leader of character, two observations:

- First, I am positive many will find the detailed approach above to be extremely structured, maybe overly so. I defend my use of this detailed approach because it is most likely a process unfamiliar to most of you. It is also about a topic highly personal and possibly difficult to talk about. Hence the structure provides an assist. (Full disclosure: in one company I had the nickname "structure freak.")

- Second, some may view this as a high-risk, low-benefit exercise. I guarantee it is neither.

Will it be worthwhile? I have zero doubts. This is an amazing gift you can give to your people. We are not talking about giving them a new character. That is impossible. We are talking about helping people make small changes at the margins of key variables that make up character.

You may be having second thoughts about the challenge and even obligation of helping another person to improve his or her character. I offer this philosophical counsel:

**"Forming characters! Whose? Our own or others?
Both. And in that momentous fact lies
the peril and responsibility of our existence."**

Elihu Burritt[7]

I am suggesting it can be a huge, life-long benefit if one of your leaders can become a little bit higher on the integrity scale, a little bit more of a team player, a little bit more respectful of people, a little bit more open in communicating, a little bit more open in receiving feedback or ideas, a little bit more honest when it is tough to be honest, a little bit more accountable for results and actions. Those are all improvements in leadership character not competency.

This could be your legacy, leader.

Chapter 7

A Premier Leader Development Institution

**"Our goal is to be the preeminent leader development institution
in the world."**

*Lieutenant General Robert L. Caslen,
Superintendent, U. S. Military Academy[1]*

This chapter presents a case study of West Point and how it develops leaders
of character.

This case study is offered not for you to emulate but rather for you to
understand and learn. It is addressed to the senior executives of a corporation
or organization who wish to establish and institutionalize a culture and a
system which develops leaders at all levels of the company. Your people may
not long recall the acquisitions, product launches, or profit margins, but
they will remember vividly if you recruited, cultivated and developed an
army of leaders. Wouldn't that be a fabulous legacy?

One of the most respected corporations in the US in the area of management
development is General Electric. It is the subject of a wonderful case study
at the Harvard Business School. GE has schools and courses at all levels,
maintains an excellent cadre of teachers at Crotonville, NY, and has a highly
praised system of preparing candidates for the top jobs.

Several years back, GE CEO Jack Welch sent a team to "benchmark" the US
Army's system of life-long leadership development. (Benchmarking refers
to looking at a specific practice or function at a good company in another
industry for ideas for improving a specific practice or function. GE also,
for instance, benchmarked Wal-Mart's distribution system.) Welch was
particularly interested in the Army's long tradition of periodically taking
officers away from the mainstream for some introspection, classes, and

interaction with peers and senior leaders. Not only are these schools highly competitive, they are required for selection to certain jobs and promotions.

However, the officer and noncommissioned officer programs in the Army, although very effective, are huge and operate at multiple posts around the country. It would be difficult to offer a case study on the total US Army system. Plus, I don't think it would serve our purpose.

Instead I would like to offer as a case study for leadership development, the United States Military Academy at West Point. I do so for four reasons. First, it has the reputation of being the premier leadership development institution in the world. Second, I am intimately familiar with it. Third, with a relatively small cadet population located at one place, it can easily be isolated and examined for lessons for other companies. And fourth, it exemplifies better than any comparable institution a focus on character, the central theme of this book.

You may ask, "Why let your background give prominence to West Point?"

I have great respect for all of the academies. Though the fierce sports competition between the service academies is legendary, they really have much more in common than they are different. But I confess that I hold West Point first among equals in leadership development for two reasons: First, West Point has been at it longer. In 1946, Chief of Staff of the Army Dwight Eisenhower wrote to the West Point Superintendent Maxwell Taylor, suggesting he establish a basic course in the curriculum on leadership.[2] Not only was it the first among the service academies, it was the first in any college in the United States. Second, in the Army, the focus of its fighting power is on the soldier, whereas the other services focus mainly on planes and ships. It is because of this focus that the Army and West Point place an unusually high premium on leadership and therefore leadership development. (The respect for and elevation of the soldier in the Army culture is demonstrated by the fact that the writing protocol throughout the entire institution requires Soldier with a capital "S.")

My intention here is not to suggest you make your firm like West Point. You couldn't do that, nor would you want to. But it will be instructive to learn principles for developing a system and a culture for maximizing leader development. So here is a case study of West Point: how it develops leaders and how you could use some of the elements of its program to develop leaders in your company.

West Point was established in 1802 at a sharp bend in the Hudson River in New York. The location gave it strategic importance during the Revolutionary War and its name.

The academy literature doesn't speak of a four-year "curriculum," which it has. West Point speaks in terms of a four-year "West Point Leadership Development System." And as with all things military, it has an acronym, "WPLDS."[3]

WPLDS rests on four pillars: **Academic**, **Physical**, **Military**, and **Character**. Unlike universities across the country where academics is the only mandated requirement, West Point spends a lot of its resources and cadet time on all four of these pillars, and all four contribute to leader development. Here is a brief overview of the four.[4]

1. The Military Academy ranks well in *academics*. West Point offers a choice of 37 majors with a core curriculum half in social sciences and humanities and half in mathematics, science, and engineering. Forbes ranked it in 2017 as the #1 Public College and the 6th best "Liberal Arts University." US News & World Report in 2016 ranked it as the #2 "Top Public College." The Princeton Review rates it routinely as the college with the "Most Accessible Professors," largely because

of such small classes and the integration of the teaching cadre into other aspects of cadet life. This is particularly relevant to leadership development, as the cadre serve as leadership role models for these officers-to-be.[5]

2. The most visible sign of the ***physical*** pillar to the American public is intercollegiate athletics. In National Collegiate Athletic Association competition, West Point has 15 men's teams and 9 women's. There are also 29 non-NCAA sports clubs such as rugby, bicycling, and boxing, which routinely bring home national titles. Those cadets not on intercollegiate sporting teams play intramural sports every semester. Moreover, every year, each cadet takes a series of core physical training classes to include a PT test and a demanding obstacle course. Monday through Thursday afternoons from 4:15 to 6:30, every cadet will be on some athletic field. It was Superintendent Douglas MacArthur, in 1920, who insisted "Every cadet an athlete."[6] He had the following carved into the stone at the entrance to the gymnasium:

"Upon the fields of friendly strife are sown the seeds
that, upon other fields, on other days
will bear the fruits of victory."

While I have not seen the data to prove it, I believe physical fitness to be an asset in virtually every leadership role, in and out of the military.

3. Most, but not all, of the ***military*** training occurs in the summer months. The cadets learn the whole array of military skills from rifle marksmanship to night patrolling. Some of the training is at a camp on the outlying West Point grounds, and some occurs at posts throughout the Army. The majority of the military training puts cadets into real leadership roles for experience, coaching, and growth. The summer training is augmented by classes on military topics during the academic year to include studying battle case studies involving recent graduates' experiences in Iraq, Afghanistan, and Africa.[7]

4. The most unique and fundamental of the four pillars is ***character***. It can be best summed up by the motto "Duty-Honor-Country." Broadly speaking, the Academy wishes to produce leaders who will

do their duty no matter how difficult, live honorably in acts and deeds, and serve faithfully in the defense of the nation. Because *character* is the theme of my book, I will return to this topic later.

It is hard to compare West Point to other colleges and universities. Except for vacations at Christmas, Easter, and one month in the summer, cadets are in this system 24/7 for four strenuous years. It is a grueling schedule. Many people do not realize that there is no college tuition at West Point. In fact, each student is actually in the US Army with a rank of "cadet." After graduation, they incur an obligation to serve as an officer for five years in the active Army and three more in the reserves. If a cadet leaves the Academy for any reason in the first two years, there is no obligation to serve.

Any cadet who leaves after the beginning of the junior year has the option either to pay a calculated amount of money for "restitution" based on how much time was spent at the Academy or to serve in the Army as an enlisted soldier.

The cadets also are paid to attend West Point. This goes largely toward books, uniforms, and other expenses. If they are thrifty, cadets will have enough for a down payment on a car their senior year. No student loans. But in reality, like all veterans, they write a blank check to the United States of America for an amount up to and including their lives.

I can recall after my graduation a man at a bar, who had imbibed a bit too much, blasting me for my free education which he said he funded as a taxpayer. I thanked him profusely for helping to pay for my education. I enlightened him as to the precise, total amount. And I informed him, "My main memory of the wonderful four-year ordeal was such that I truly believed I had been forced to ingest that entire sum via a most indelicate part of my anatomy, nickel by nickel." That shut him up for a while.

West Point is certainly one of most famous institutions in the world. In the past decade, Chinese visitors have flocked to West Point in huge numbers.

Puzzled, I asked one such visitor, a member of the Chinese Communist Party, "Why do so many Chinese want to see West Point and no other institutions?"

His reply: "In World War II, West Pointers saved the world—Eisenhower in Europe and MacArthur in the Pacific."[8]

An overstatement to be sure, but it makes the point that West Point has an international reputation for leadership development. It is often said that West Point has produced great leaders for our country. Frequently cited are

Lee, Grant, Pershing, MacArthur, Patton, Arnold, Bradley, Eisenhower, Taylor, and Schwarzkopf.

I believe the true litmus test for greatness is not the recognizable names of Generals, Presidents, and CEOs, but the fact that each year, now for over two centuries, West Point has produced young Second Lieutenants who are very good leaders, who strive to accomplish difficult missions, and who take care of their troops. Hard to measure with numbers, but the batting average for graduating solid leaders is very high. I can't say 100%, but it is close.

As a young man in high school, I was fairly bright, a good athlete, quite sociable and outgoing, but I had a dreadful hatred of standing and reciting in front of the class. When called to read a pretty good essay I had written, my hands would shake, and I would turn scarlet. I don't know why, but I was overly self-conscious in front of a group. For a lot of reasons I always wanted to go to West Point. One of the reasons was that I simply hated myself for this deficit in my own confidence, and I knew West Point would correct this. It did, very quickly.

The first day at West Point I had to learn to recite the answer to this question: "What are the only answers a plebe can give?"

Since my time years ago, "Ma'am" and "Sergeant" have been added after the "Sir" to recognize the full integration of women into West Point and the Army and the fairly recent addition of Noncommissioned Officers who now play a large role in assisting the tactical officers in bringing up the cadets.

The required response (in a very loud voice):

- **"Yes, Sir/Ma'am/Sergeant"**
- **"No, Sir/Ma'am/Sergeant"**
- **"No Excuse, Sir/Ma'am/Sergeant"**
- **"Sir/Ma'am/Sergeant, I do not understand"**

Read again the third answer from the list above. Imagine that, within hours of joining, the cadet is required to voice the premise of being accountable for actions and not making excuses. To the extent that this holds for a career or a lifetime, isn't that a marvelous instillation of a simply outstanding character value! I suggest that managers at all levels in business today would be delighted with people on their team who refrain from offering excuses.

As a plebe, I had to memorize and shout arcane bits of trivia about West Point.[9] Should an upperclassman ask how many gallons of water are in Lusk Reservoir, my answer:

"Sir, there are 78 million gallons
when the water is flowing over the spillway."

And an old favorite I will never forget: "What is the definition of leather?"

"If the fresh skin of an animal, cleaned and divested of
all hair, fat, and other extraneous matter,
be immersed in a dilute solution of tannic acid,
a chemical combination ensues;
the gelatinous tissue of the skin is converted
into a non putrescible substance,
impervious to and insoluble in water;
this sir is leather."

Some instructors in leadership class have started using this seemingly ridiculous definition as a metaphor for the leader development process: "Is West Point trying to make young men and women into non putrescible leaders of character?" I take that to mean "tough." (And recall tough is character not competency.) Not sure about the tannic acid.

It is thought that some plebe in a previous century had been asked a bona fide question which caused the plebe to do the research. Heaven only knows how accurate the answer was, but it has been passed down nevertheless and is now part of the rich tradition. And all answers had to be exact, loud, and forceful. Fanciful, maybe ludicrous, but this process forced the plebe to memorize and recite in a loud voice under great pressure. Perform, produce, under pressure. Any habit of hesitation due to self-consciousness was eroded and eventually destroyed.

Similarly, I was required regularly to "call the minutes." Standing in the barracks hall at attention, I announced the uniform for the next formation, the menu for the meal about to be served, and what movie was showing on the weekend. I would begin this drill at either 5 or 10 minutes prior to the formation time and call out this recitation every minute at the top of my lungs. Again—perform, produce, under pressure. No time to be self-conscious. Just loud, accurate, and on time.

Every day for four years I was required to recite in almost every class. This forced me to communicate to the instructor and to a group of peers clearly and with persuasion on every conceivable subject. This daily recital goes back to Sylvanus Thayer, West Point's superintendent (1817-1839), who developed the foundational educational system that undergirds West Point. Throughout the four years, there is at West Point an emphasis on clear, concise, and accurate communication, both oral and written—an absolute essential for a good leader.

I had long thought of marching, or the antiquated term "dismounted drill," as a means to instill discipline and order into a military unit. It requires concentration and precision of movement both as an individual and as a unit. It can build teamwork, cohesion, and pride.

Marching is also is a superb leadership training exercise. I had to learn to give the correct commands, at the correct time, and on the correct foot while marching. Standing in front of a formation of cadets (or soldiers) and giving an order is a parade-ground rehearsal for a later leadership task of giving an order for what could be a life or death situation. And as leadership author Jim Collins wrote, "In business, if you make bad decisions, people lose money, and perhaps jobs. In the military, if you make bad decisions, nations can fall and people can die."[10]

All of these activities, plus giving classes to younger cadets as I progressed, forced me to get in front of others and to speak. I didn't realize it at the time but this practice markedly changed my self-confidence and my self-identity. I became a leader.

In the vast leadership literature, I do not think communication in general, and public speaking in particular, has gotten ample credit for leadership development. Who can lead who cannot speak?

And I am not talking about communication skills, like how to deliver a speech, conduct a performance evaluation, or organize a conference call. I refer to these as leadership communications *competencies*. I am really talking about an attitude within the leader that he or she has something worthy of presenting and the inclination and willingness to say it. This confidence and willingness to speak up is clearly a leadership *character* trait. (Recall this key distinction earlier in Chapter 3.)

The development of a self-concept of a leader is perhaps the most critical step of all for character development. If some people do not think of themselves as leaders, guess what— they're not.

West Point has the very distinct advantage of being able to correctly promise cadets that after graduation they will be in charge of twenty to forty soldiers.

There is no question of whether or not a cadet will be in a leadership role; the only question is whether or not the cadet will be a good leader. So, the self-concept of being a leader is very fundamentally instilled from day one. Knowing that a person will be in a leadership role, possibly combat, is instrumental in conveying to the young cadet that he or she had better well be a leader, and a good one.

Many scholars who have focused on leadership development believe the formulation of a self-image as a leader and the ability to project that self-concept into future, larger roles of leadership is absolutely critical to leadership development. "The development of leadership skills is inextricably integrated with the development of the person's self-concept or identity as a leader."[11]

I believe the singular achievement of the West Point's four-year program is to graduate virtually 100% who know they are leaders and aspire to be not just leaders but very good leaders. This ranks well above any and all leadership skills learned there. Again, *character* over *competency*.

Character has been integral to the Military Academy since its founding.[12]

The word "character" has been in either the Academy's mission or purpose statement at least since 1950. But it was in 1988 that Superintendent David Palmer joined the words *leadership* and *character* and incorporated the combined phrase in redefining the purpose of West Point: "To provide the Nation with *leaders of character* who serve the common defense." [Emphasis added.][13]

This phrase "leaders of character" has prevailed since then and is central to the current mission statement of West Point.[14]

> **"To educate, train, and inspire the Corps of Cadets**
> **so that each graduate is a commissioned leader of character**
> **committed to the values of Duty, Honor, Country**
> **and prepared for a career of professional excellence**
> **and service to the nation as an officer in the U.S. Army."[15]**

This change was not just wordsmithing. General Palmer refocused his team on the primacy of the concept of "leaders of character." And he enjoined the entire staff to be part of developing leaders of character. It took a series of meetings and more than a year, but it manifested both a bold and profound change. It shouts to the world that West Point will develop "leaders of character" with the understanding that it expects the country to hold it accountable for doing just that.

It is instructive to compare this mission statement with those of the following elite business schools:

- <u>Harvard</u>: "to educate *leaders* who make a difference in the world."

- <u>Stanford</u>: "to develop innovative, principled, and insightful *leaders* who improve the world."

- <u>Dartmouth</u>: "…[preparing] students for *leadership* positions in the world's foremost organizations."

- <u>MIT</u>: "to develop principled, innovative *leaders* who improve the world."[16]

And "leadership" seems to also pop up outside of the business schools as evidenced by these other highly esteemed <u>Harvard</u> schools:

- <u>Law</u>: "To educate *leaders* who contribute to the development of justice and the wellbeing of society."

- <u>Medical</u> "To create and nurture a diverse community of the best people committed to *leadership* in alleviating suffering caused by disease."

- <u>Divinity</u> "to educate women and men for service as *leaders* in religious life and thought."

- <u>Government</u>: "to train enlightened public *leaders*."

- <u>Education</u>: "to prepare *leaders* in education and to generate knowledge."[17]

I was frankly surprised to discover that all of these very prestigious schools had "leaders" or "leadership" in their mission statements. This was a revelation for me. I had just assumed that institutions of higher learning would have educational goals and not focus on leadership. I was wrong.

It is an ironic twist that the word "leader" seems ubiquitous in these mission statements but plays such a small and ill-thought-of role in the curricula. I find it astounding that leading academics at these institutions do not believe these institutions can prove that they deliver leaders.

Recall in Chapter 2, I reviewed a fairly extensive self-critique of their results. One succinct quote from three Harvard Business School professors is repeated here: "Virtually all of the top business schools aspire to 'develop leaders,' yet their efforts in this area are widely viewed as falling short."[18]

And none of the above schools even pretend to develop "leaders of character" as does West Point.

An interesting hypothesis: It may be that the problem generally accepted by top academics that their leadership research, doctrine, and instruction is ineffective is precisely because the character component is not included.

Not only does West Point include the component of character, it has given it prominence. It underscores all else at the institution. It is enabled to do so because it has a student body under its tutelage 24-7. Moreover, the values it instills are drawn from a very purposeful Army Code of Professional Military Ethics and the Academy motto of "Duty-Honor-Country." The other academic institutions are unable to narrow their focus on values they wish to promote as can the Military Academy. Hence the other schools would be hard pressed to come up with a universal set of character traits that define character.

The Military Academy's energies were refocused in 2013, when Superintendent Robert L. Caslen, Jr. arrived. He took a reasonably well-defined program designed to develop character and added clarity around aspects of a person's life that could be considered *off duty*. "The American people and our soldiers expect us to behave honorably and inspirationally all the time…they do not make a distinction between private life and public life, even if we believe that distinction exists."[19]

After extensive review and collaboration by his leadership team, Caslen broadened the character approach as follows:

West Point Facets of Character:
• **Performance: duty, resilience, and grit necessary to accomplish the mission and get results** • **Leadership: establishing a safe, positive, command climate where everyone thrives awhile achieving results** • **Moral: assess the moral-ethical aspects of every situation and take appropriate action regardless of consequences** • **Civic: treat others with respect and display selflessness** • **Social: proper decorum in all professional, social, and online environments.**[20]

Caslen has succeeded in focusing all departments and offices at West Point on supporting this "leaders of character" mission. Leadership development is not just the role of the tactical officers, but that of every instructor, staff officer, noncommissioned officer, and civilian on post. Moreover, the different functions across the organizational spectrum are integrated in such a way as to streamline and align the process in order to minimize cadet confusion and maximize effectiveness. A headline in one of the Academy manuals is a challenge to all:

> **"Every interaction [with a cadet]
> is a developmental opportunity."[21]**

Here is a story which I hope will exemplify this.

Several years ago, a cadet turned in a required report a day late, something I am led to believe happens rarely. I can only imagine that the same paper in any other school would be nicked a grade for tardiness or the error overlooked entirely. At West Point, the instructor not only took off a few points, but also asked to talk to the cadet after class.

Picture this instructor in her West Point classroom. She had graduated from the Academy ten years earlier, fought in Afghanistan, received a Master's degree in English from Columbia, wore the rank of Major, and was now serving along with her many colleagues as a role model for the cadets. More importantly, she felt it her role to coach this cadet after class, not on the content of the paper but on a key component of character. The "Duty" part of the cadet motto means you get the job done, well, and on time. The most important lesson this English teacher taught that day was not in English composition; it was in character composition.

Thus, all members of the faculty and staff at West Point support in some way the challenging and audacious goal to make all graduates "leaders of character." The team includes professors, instructors, tactical officers and noncommissioned officers, coaches and staff. It would surprise me if the contingent of military police on campus has not been asked how they can assist.

Leadership roles change over the four years at West Point. Generally, in the first-year cadets are learning how to follow. Some describe it as learning how to lead oneself, although there are opportunities to lead others. In the second-year cadets are responsible for a few plebes. In the third-year cadets are responsible for leading larger teams. And in the last year, cadets form the cadre to lead the entire corps of cadets.

The process has been refined over the years, but it comports to theories and findings of experts in the academic field of developmental psychology. Leadership is developed over the four years with a series of increasing leadership roles, robust coaching and feedback, introspection, and learning.

Psychologist Robert Kegan has authored a highly accepted model of how personality and character are developed over several stages. When applied to West Point's process of developing a sense of honor as defined by the honor code, the model demonstrates how honor is internalized by the cadets. The same applies to all other values, but let us examine honor using Kegan's concept.

The cadet doesn't just automatically "become honorable" on the first day at West Point, standing at attention with right hand raised and swearing allegiance to the Constitution, although that is a very important event and rite of passage. It takes time and effort to develop, deepen, and internalize the character trait of *honor*.

It is assumed that cadets enter West Point with a certain level of honor, developed from home, family, schools and communities (Stage 1). Then this value construct of honor is internalized over the cadet's time at West Point, going through stages 2, 3, and 4.[22]

Stage 2	Stage 3	Stage 4
Honor as something imposed; compliance for fear of losing opportunity or reputation	Honor is owed to the group; as the basis for trust	Honor is personally defined; manifested in all roles

A major reason that West Point can be so successful in doing the above is because USMA is precisely what Sociologist Erving Goffman described as a "total institution." This is an institution in which a person is completely immersed in the environment which controls every aspect of day-to-day life under a singular authority. Virtually everything is prescribed down to how you fold your laundry and what shelf it goes on. West Point is an institution which alters a way of living and in so doing indoctrinates the cadets to accept norms and values of the Academy and the Army.[23]

Cadets and graduates alike might not take kindly to the fact that Goffman's concept was developed by studying an insane asylum in Washington, DC. But West Point as a total institution provides the mechanism to adjust and shape a person's attitudes, values and character in a very positive manner. This of course is one aspect of leadership development in a major organization which most likely would be hard to apply to your firm or agency.

The honor code is so integral to West Point and to the development of character that I need to elaborate on it.

The honor concept goes back to the founding days with Sylvanus Thayer circa 1820 when a cadet was always expected to tell the truth and a cadet's word was always accepted. Superintendent Douglas MacArthur, a century later in 1920, added measurably by establishing an honor committee and codifying the Honor Code.[24] Graduates (some very famous) refer to the code and motto as the essence of the Academy:

"What the Academy stands for, has always been my guide throughout my military career, and to have approached the high ideals of duty, honor, and service to country that are the real spirit of West Point has to me a meaning that nothing else has. The longer I live, the further I have gone in the Service, the more I reverence the things that inspire the heart and soul… at West Point."

General of the Armies John J. "Blackjack" Pershing, USMA class of 1886.[25]

"West Point gives its graduates something that far transcends the techniques and knowledge involved in developing, training, and leading an army. It helps them build character, integrity. This quality is more easily sensed than descried, more readily felt than discussed, but at West Point it is as real as the honor code. Character is the Academy's overriding concern, a concern to which it has always given single-minded, almost fanatical devotion. It is because of this that West Point is hailed by military institutions throughout the world."

General of the Army Dwight D. Eisenhower, USMA class of 1915.[26]

The edict on this wall is not just a combination of nice words on a monument. It is a belief and a value statement deeply embedded into day-to-day activities and classes:

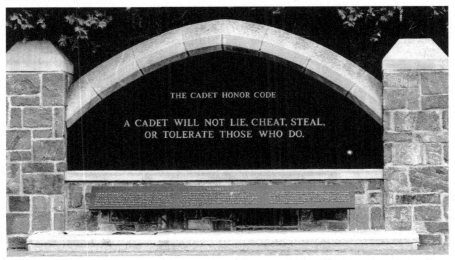

Park bench adjacent to the cadet barracks

The "no tolerance clause" really sets this honor code apart from others, and it is expected and demanded during cadet days and after graduation. Most Academy graduates will vouch for the belief that the West Point honor code is very real, totally supported, and separates this school from others. Every cadet is expected to make a truthful statement and to receive one as well—always.

"My word is my bond."

West Point has had its share of painful honor scandals, one in 1951 and another in 1976, both plagued by a failure of a large contingent of cadets to report honor violations. But the code has survived and since grown stronger. Assuming some of the blame for these tragedies, the Academy has made changes to the honor system and to various academic systems to minimize the temptation for cheating.[27]

I truly believe that a very high level of honor and integrity in the Corps of Cadets is the standard today. Cheating is simply not tolerated.

This is not the case in most schools. The Center for Academic Integrity at the LBJ School of Public Affairs reports, "In most college campuses, 70 percent of undergraduate students admit to some cheating."[28] Another researcher writes, "According to surveys, between two-thirds and three-quarters of high school and university students admit to some cheating within the past year."[29]

And in one college, students were recently caught cheating in an ethics class![30] (Did somebody not get the memo?)

I was surprised to learn that MBA students cheat at a higher rate than other grad students (engineering, education, or law).[31] I speculate that in MBA programs, grades can largely determine salaries after graduation and that classroom competition is fierce. Most of the Baker Scholars (roughly top 5%) from Harvard go to top consulting or investment banking firms for big bucks.[32]

Some discomforting research on academic cheating suggests that cheating may be associated with dishonesty later in life. College students who cheated (plagiarized) reported themselves more likely to break rules in the workplace, cheat on spouses, and engage in illegal activities. And high schoolers who cheat on exams reported themselves significantly more likely to lie to a customer, inflate an insurance claim, lie to or deceive their boss, or cheat on their taxes.[33] This gives credence to the notion that values and ethics formed in colleges follow the student (or cadet) after graduation.

At West Point, a very significant aspect of the leader of character goes beyond the Cadet Honor Code (no lying, stealing, or cheating) and draws from the motto, "Duty-Honor-Country." It speaks to serving the country honorably by doing one's duty well.

The following mandate comes from the Cadet Prayer:

**"Make us to choose the harder right
instead of the easier wrong."[34]**

I personally did not grasp the power of this quote until long after graduation. It has application far and wide. There are examples, some very recent, where senior officers have not lived up to this goal. But it clearly is the ideal, and most graduates follow it throughout life. West Point has deeply embedded it into its value system and its culture.

In recent years a cadet creed has been added to the character development regimen. Cadets now learn and recite the following cadet creed. It sums up the values of West Point to include the honor code. And it places the cadet development process under the larger aegis of the professionalism of the US Army.

The Cadet Creed

**"As a future officer, I am committed to the values of
Duty, Honor and Country.**

**I am an aspiring member of the Army Profession,
dedicated to serve and earn the trust of the American people.**

It is my duty to maintain the honor of the Corps.

**I will live above the common level of life,
And have the courage to choose the harder right over the easier wrong.**

**I will live with honor and integrity,
scorn injustice, and confront substandard behavior.**

I will persevere through adversity and recover from failure.

**I will embrace the warrior ethos,
and pursue excellence in everything I do.**

I am a future officer and a member of the Long Gray Line."

Of course, being honorable is not a new idea:

**"To see what is right, and not to do it,
is want of courage or of principle."**

Confucius

And Mark Twain always puts a unique spin on things:

**"Always do right.
This will gratify some people, and astonish the rest."**

Mark Twain

To be sure, it is often difficult to *do the harder right instead of the easier wrong.*
But what is often overlooked is that it can also be a challenge to distinguish
between right and wrong. In many cases, values will be competing and the
solution may be both complex and difficult.

Years ago, I wrote in an article on military ethics that is applicable today:

"Far too many officers resolve dilemmas only in the heat of crisis
and emotion. The crisis can derive from social pressure or from the

heat of battle, neither of which maximizes rational analysis and predictable behavior so essential to conducting the business of war...

"If the specific ethical issues were discussed and analyzed before the frenzy of pressure for a decision arrived, individual and group strength for supporting "correct action" would be enhanced."...

"Ethical issues are seldom either black or white; they occur in the gray zone... Our goal should be not to eliminate the gray but to illuminate it."[35]

This is exactly what West Point is doing now and is an integral part of character development. They use a particular methodology called the Leader Challenge Approach which involves the presentation of case studies of real challenges faced by recent graduates. The cadets discuss principles that apply and debate several options. According to one officer, "When we immerse ourselves in the tough, real-life challenge of another leader, we hone our judgment and we grow more prepared for our own future challenges." [36]

A common theme is whether to do what you have been told to do or to do what you believe is right. This conundrum can take many forms, none easy to resolve. The process of discussing these real (not fabricated) issues with peers, doing some personal soul searching, and making a case for a solution are all part of formulating and strengthening a set of values.

In addition to this leader challenge program, The West Point William E. Simon Center for the Professional Military Ethic, sponsors twenty-three, cadet-facilitated seminars on honor, sexual harassment and assault, and other civic, social, and moral facets of character.[37]

It is important to note that these seminars are led by cadet leaders with guidance and supervision from the faculty. The program is designed to develop leaders of character in front of the class as well as in the seats.

The West Point curriculum has included a mandatory course in leadership since 1948. A new three-credit course has recently been added for seniors, "Officership, the Superintendent's Capstone Course." It entails an integrative approach using a lot of the material cadets have been exposed to in their past three years to solve complex problems they will likely face as officers.[38] Another recent development is the "Special Leader Development Programs for Honor, Respect, and Alcohol." When cadets fall short of USMA's expectations in terms of character, they enter into a highly structured and supervised development experience with a mentor. This again underscores the Academy's belief that character is developed and that the institution can have a significant role in steering that process.[39]

I liken WPLDS to a well-orchestrated surround-sound system, where the music comes not just from the front but from the sides, the ceiling, the floor, the back. It is supported by everyone on the post. It is the overarching goal of this total institution. The music (message) of this surround-sound system is played in class, in the barracks, on the parade field, at the gym, and on the rifle range. The values that make up the character component are emblazoned all over.

"Duty Honor Country" is inscribed on the stain glass window at the front of the cadet chapel. It is on every class ring. (Dating from well before the Civil War, the West Point class ring was the first ring in American schools. Many graduates donate their rings at death to the ingot from which the new class molds its rings, thus symbolizing the linkage of past classes to the present.) The motto is also inscribed on the Academy crest.

The WPLDS draws from the rich heritage of West Point to deepen its values. Statues and monuments of its famous heroes are all over the place. Traditions abound.

The bugle calls, parades, and music all reinforce basic values of this profession serving the nation with honor.

From "The Alma Mater":

> **"Let Duty be well performed.**
> **Honor be e'er untarned.**
> **Country be ever armed.**
> **West Point, by thee."**[40]

From the 1910 Hymn "The Corps!"

> **"The Corps! Bareheaded salute it,**
> **With eyes up, thanking our God —**
> **That we of the Corps are treading**
> **Where they of the Corps have trod...**
> **Grips hands tho' it be from the shadows —**
> **While we swear, as you did of yore,**
> **Or living, or dying, to honor**
> **The Corps, and the Corps, and the Corps."**[41]

The eyes of tradition watch over these cadets from what is called the Long Gray Line. Scores of alumni at well attended reunions watch over the young officer candidates with careful eye and clouded memories. I recall that the cadet gray came from the color of the uniforms worn by General Winfield Scott and his soldiers when they defeated the British in Canada in the summer of 1814. I used to think the famous "long gray line" referred to cadets wearing the same cadet gray for over two centuries. Alas, only recently at a reunion of my class did I discover that the long gray line is called that because we are all so gray.

Thus, I conclude my somewhat biased account of West Point, the world's premier leadership development institution. A more comprehensive culture for the integration of character and leadership development is nowhere to be found. While it is true that such a culture cannot be replicated in a business setting, I know firsthand that understanding West Point's ideals and system can help guide the transformation of a company to a focus on character-centered leadership.

In the next chapter, we will draw lessons from this case study and lay out a template for you to place leadership development into your company's DNA.

Chapter 8

How to Create a Company of Leaders

"Maybe not every day, but some day when you least expect it, every soldier in this outfit has to be ready to be a leader, and a damned good one."
Lieutenant Colonel Ernie Webb[1]

I have offered West Point as a case study because I believe it is the gold standard as the world's premier leadership development institution and especially because it has "leaders of character" as its primary goal. Now the question is, "What can you learn from the West Point case study and apply it to your company, agency, or nonprofit organization?"

What you can *learn* is different from what can you *copy*. Just because of the fundamental nature of USMA, there is little that you could or would want to copy. But there are concepts and principles employed at West Point that are applicable elsewhere— probably in your organization.

This presumes a real desire on your part to learn how to create a system and a culture in your company that develops leaders. Perhaps your firm or institution could earn the reputation (as some have) for being known as a leadership factory, taking in good raw material at all levels and shaping those people into solid leadership talent. This is a huge task, a major institutional shift, and a long-term undertaking. And, it would be a tremendous legacy. Think about this as your own legacy as the leader of your company, organization, or institution. Worthwhile? Read on.

By necessity and as I have stated earlier, I will shy away from the broader topic of total leadership development which goes into diagnostic metrics, assignment options, skill level descriptions, career paths, special schooling for individual leadership positions, and a lot more. I will narrow the discussion to enhancing the *character* component among your leaders at all levels, which is the topic of this book. I believe that is where there is the greatest need.

I also think a relatively small effort in this area can produce tremendous results. Character development is the trim tab to setting a course for great leadership.

At the outset, let me presume your firm or organization most likely already has much to build on. Think in terms of how to focus, align, and enhance your systems, structure, and culture. This will make the task easier and the changes more palatable. I see three broad areas where examining the West Point experience can be helpful.

Gain top leadership commitment.

West Point's superintendents made a huge effort to get all their top leadership on board, first with the addition of "leader of character" into its mission by General Palmer in 1988, and again in 2013 with the current superintendent's initiatives. This wasn't a one-man mandate. It was in both cases more of a top team discussion, debate, and analysis. The discussions occurred over weeks and months and served to get all members on board.

As they did, you should make this organizational change initiative a **team effort**. The organizational goal of introducing a character-focused leadership development program has to be owned by the top leadership team, not just the CEO. The top leader of course has to be committed, but so also does the top team of executives or leaders. If that commitment is not solid, you will be wasting money, time, and effort.

I emphasize getting your top executive team committed to this effort because it is more important than getting their consensus on strategy, product design, or mergers, for instance. To make the introduction of a character focused leader development program take root, your leaders don't just have to buy into it, they have to role model and lead it. It is more than intellectual commitment to apply resources toward an objective. It entails a very personal commitment to live it.

Often an outside consultant might help this teaming effort. The best I know is my old firm, the Senn-Delaney Leadership Consulting Company. I draw much insight presented in this chapter from my past work with them and their clients.

On one assignment, I was tasked to support Pat Donahue, at the time CEO of McDonald's of Canada. He realized he had major divisions in his company, East vs. West and company staff vs. franchisees. A superb leader, he worked tirelessly to change the mindset and attitudes of his top team and managers.

His commitment and involvement was crucial. He was personally engaged in leading a series of workshops we conducted across Canada. His buy-in and commitment fueled the program.

When asked if he got a return on the culture consulting work we did for him, his answer was, "Over the several years, all of our key metrics were turned significantly in the right direction. Most likely there were many reasons for this. But I will tell you that some key decisions, which we were able to get everyone to support and which previously we could not, were directly responsible for net earnings more than doubling the cost of the consulting initiative."[2]

Watching Pat lead this effort, I marveled at his ability to lead by example and show the company the values desired for the reshaped culture. I also had a major insight which became a key premise of this book:

The cultural values a company wishes its people to conform to are identical to leadership character traits the company wishes all its leaders to buy into.

Company Cultural Values	=	Leadership Character Traits

If you wish your people to work and live with integrity, it is the same thing as wishing your leaders to lead with integrity. The same can be said of other values such as respecting others, being a good team player, being open and honest in your communication, being accountable, and other qualities.

Similarly, "guiding behaviors" which provide specific detail for each value in your company culture can also provide detail for traits in your leadership character. Here is an example:

	Desired Culture For All Employees	**Desired Character Trait For Leaders**
Example Value	Integrity	Integrity
Example Guiding Behaviors	Don't lie. Don't cheat. Don't steal.	Don't lie. Don't cheat. Don't steal.

The company cultural values and the leader character traits use the same language. The only difference is that the cultural values are defined to show how people should act in the company, whereas the character traits are the platform for more effective and stronger leadership. By living these values, the leaders will build *trust* with their teams which will increase their ability to *influence* their followers. Ergo better *leadership*.

This linkage seems pretty basic. But because this is a text about character traits of leaders and how to improve them, this construct is significant. It means that if your firm has progressed in defining your desired culture, you are already down the path of improving the character component of your leaders, which by definition includes you.

Thus, if you have a start in any kind of initiative related to your corporate values and culture, as most organizations have, you are off and running with the start (at least) of a leadership development program.

In defining the values and guiding behaviors you deem appropriate for your company's culture, you are defining the character traits for leaders at all levels for your leader development system.

Please note this is a different approach from that used in Chapter 4, which described how to define your own personal character traits along with guiding behaviors and from that used in Chapter 6, which described how to help people on your team carve out their own personal character traits and guiding behaviors. Those were self-generated and focused on the individual. Now across the entire company, for leader development you are being prescriptive with one set of values and guiding behaviors.

You share an advantage with West Point in having a particular and tailored set of values for all to emulate. Theirs supports a professional military ethic; yours is tailored for and supports your business and company mission. MBA schools across the country do not have this luxury as their graduates are heading in all directions to all types of companies each with its own unique culture and values.

To reiterate, the effort to retool your current program, activities, and culture requires an unusual level of commitment by the top leadership team. It requires leading by example, which means living your values and working to improve your own leadership character. It takes a real leader to make this happen—a bold leader.

I once thought the firm or organization attempting a transformational program like this had to be quite *large* to have the resources to apply to this effort. But I now think *bold* is more important than *large*. The right mindset and committed actions can occur in a company of literally any size—or not.

I worked with a company of 180 employees that had instituted what they called a "university." Having just attended a two-week course for executives at "Bank One College," I thought "university" was a little over the top for this small company. But being bold and creative was common in this firm. For example, striving for feedback from their end user customers, they printed a 1-800 customer service telephone number on every one of their specialty light bulbs.[3]

Examine your company *culture* and improve on it.

West Point has a very unique culture that combines strong tradition with a focus on leadership. Its leaders examine and shape continuously all aspects of the cadet's waking hours to insure nothing impedes the development of these leaders of character. It is a culture that supports the time-tested honor code.

It is a culture that places a very high premium on leading by example, introspection, and mentoring. It presents opportunities for cadets to speak in stressful situations, and to assume leadership roles of expanding importance. It promotes learning from experience from increasingly responsible positions. Every aspect of the academy is honed to insure it supports their overarching goal of developing leaders of character.

Against that backdrop, I encourage you to examine your firm's corporate culture. This discussion about culture is directly linked to the development of your leadership development system. Let's start with some basics about culture.

Culture itself is not a new term. It comes from sociology and anthropology and includes a society's art, literature, lifestyles, value systems, traditions, rituals, and beliefs. The main purpose of values is to define the desired culture. Edgar Schein writes, "The culture of a group can be defined as the accumulated shared learning of that group…which has worked well enough to be considered valid and, therefore, taught to new members as the correct way to perceive, think, feel and behave..."[4]

The concept of *socialization* happens when individuals learn about and adapt to the norms and values of the culture they join. In some organizations, this is a well thought out process starting with an employee orientation built around values of the firm. In others, it is happenstance. In any event, socialization is the teaching of new group members the values which define the culture.[5]

The concept of a *subculture* is also a fundamental term in this academic field. It pertains to a subgroup within a society, such as the medical profession, academia, the military, or a prison population. The subculture is similar to the larger culture in a lot of ways, but it is also unique to the smaller group or segment of society. My first look at subculture was via a book by my sociology professor at Northwestern who wrote in the 1960's about the drug subculture in America.[6]

In the 1980's, a number of academics led by Edgar Schein argued that each company has its own unique subculture.[7] In 1982, Deal and Kennedy wrote a bestselling book, *Corporate Cultures*.[8] The term "business culture" was hatched. This was to say that the culture of one business can be very distinct from that of another, even in the same industry. Simply put, the business culture is, "how people do things around here."

Often this sort of thing is covered in some form of new employee or manager orientation program. But more often than not, it is conveyed personally by coworkers as they help bring the new hire on board. Many times these "rules" are unwritten.

You may be among a group today that just does not think culture is that important. Many view this notion of business culture as too soft and squishy, hard to define or describe, virtually impossible to change, and therefore meaningless. With respect, I disagree.[9]

Stories abound about mergers between industrial giants where the numbers made sense but the cultures were antithetical. Often cited is the not-so-successful marriage between Time Warner and America-On-Line. The merger logic included complementary financials, customers, and systems but failed to take into account two company cultures about as different as can be imagined. The marriage failed.

A number of academics and others picked up on the idea and argued that a very healthy business culture could reap bottom line financial benefits. John Kotter and James Haskett in 1992 wrote, "Corporate culture can have a significant impact on a firm's long-term economic performance.... Firms with cultures that emphasized all the key managerial constituencies (customers, stock holders, and employees) and leadership from managers at all levels outperformed firms that did not have those cultural traits by a huge margin."[10]

They reported a huge difference between two categories of companies with good and poor cultures over an eleven-year period:[11]

Revenue Growth	682%	vs	166%
Employment Growth	282%	vs	36%
Stock Price Growth	901%	vs	74%
Tax Base (Net Income) Growth	756%	vs	1%

While this was a seminal study, it revealed the difficulty of defining what is a "strong and positive" culture. It also laid out the challenge to senior leadership to take responsibility for modifying or enhancing the business culture.

You have to start with, "How can you define an individual company's culture?" The answer to this is necessary so you can measure and improve it.

The best way I have seen to describe culture is with a list (5-7) of values as shown below. My experience is more than that will confuse and overload efforts to focus and improve.[12]

Example Values	
Integrity	Tenacity
Accountability	Respect
Collaboration	Creativity

For each company, there will be different values. And each of these terms called values can and will have many definitions. This can be very confusing. For instance, a company that wants to create a good culture may be espousing a set of values, including "accountability." But accountability can mean a host of things to different people and to different organizations.

To spell out accountability, it helps to describe that value with (5-7) *guiding behaviors*. If care and thought go into this, the guiding behaviors will give more detail and specifics to the value. The guiding behaviors are observable and together portray what it is like to be accountable.[13]

Here is an example of how one company defined accountability:

Guiding Behaviors for Accountability
1. We accept individual and team responsibility for our actions and results.
2. We proactively identify and address threats and barriers.
3. We lead the changes necessary to capitalize on opportunities.
4. We are willing to openly admit to mistakes.
5. We refuse to explain sub-standard results with excuses.

It should be underscored that this culture, these values, and these guiding behaviors are what the company wants to be, not what it necessarily is. It is something to shoot for. In that sense, the values and guiding behaviors are aspirational and hopefully inspirational.[14]

Notice how this process gets more specific and measurable as you go from a value to its guiding behaviors. If you take your set of values and create for each value a small number of guiding behaviors, this verbiage can easily be converted to a one-page document. It can then become a survey to find out how it's going.

Many pundits argue that culture cannot be measured: it is simply too soft. I disagree. I am presenting a measurement instrument whereby a company asks managers, employees, or customers how they rate the culture.

This survey instrument can give senior management a measured reading on where the company stands with regard to their desired culture. The survey can be repeated to track progress over time. The data can be segmented by group or organization within the corporation. If appropriate, you can measure the perspective of different levels.

To demonstrate this use, I have included on the next page a snapshot of one such survey from a company I worked with. The company had six values each detailed with its own guiding behaviors. The survey data was consolidated by groups (officers, managers, franchisees). The comparison of the group data was of keen interest to the executives. The survey was repeated periodically to measure improvement. This blunts the objection often heard with discussions of culture that if you can't measure something, you can't change it.

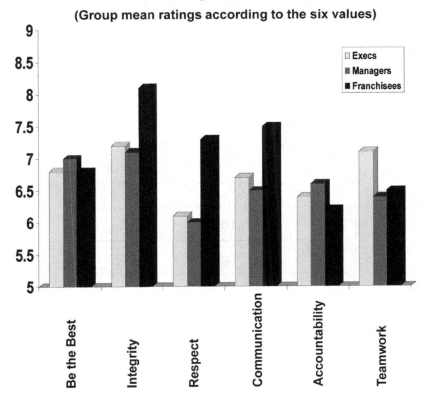

Survey of Culture

(Group mean ratings according to the six values)

With this background on the nature of culture and how to measure it, please craft your own values and guiding behaviors. Or you may wish to just reexamine what you already have.

But be cautious. Take the following example set of values: *Communication. Respect. Integrity. Excellence.*

Sounds great. A company with the right mindset and commitment, right?

This was Enron before it crashed and sent its top leadership to jail for criminal activities. Words on a paper or a billboard mean nothing if those words have no real meaning in the hearts and minds of the employees and especially the senior executives.[15]

As Patrick Lencioni warns, "Most values statements are bland, toothless, or just plain dishonest. And far from being harmless, as some executives assume, they're often highly destructive. Empty values statements create cynical and dispirited employees, alienate customers, and undermine managerial credibility."[16]

So, the first task is to check out your list of values and see if they set off the "BS" meter. If they do, start over. The values have to be real, relevant, timely, and helpful. And you must own them.

If you need to start over or check yours out, here are a few to consider:

Alibaba[17]	
Customer First	Integrity
Teamwork	Passion
Embrace Change	Commitment

IBM[18]		
Win	Execute	Team

Charlotte (FL) High School[19]	
Preparation	Determination
Respect	Excellence
Integrity	

And here is an example that goes back to 1940 when Forest Mars Sr. formed M&M Ltd.

M&Ms[20]	
Quality	Efficiency
Responsibility	Freedom
Mutuality	

Now I make the assumption that you have read the foregoing, scanned the examples, and validated or reshaped what you wish for your company culture.

And if your culture/values description was ill-defined, not specific to your firm, or something that could be regarded as lofty or meaningless, I trust you have redone it. And by adding guiding behaviors to each value, you have made it specific and meaningful for you and all your employees. You have defined with considerable precision exactly how you want people to act in your company. This is your desired culture.

This set of values, each with a corresponding set of guiding behaviors, will serve as the bedrock for not only your culture but also your leader development program.

You will note that this is the identical format covered for individuals in Chapter 4, which was called *Desired Character Profile*. The only difference is this time you prescribed a set of values for all leaders in the company, whereas in the earlier chapter, one defined a leader value set for individual application.

The Military Academy has masterfully over the years enveloped their culture with what I refer to as "surround sound." Surveying the beautiful campus at West Point, a visitor or a cadet sees nothing that doesn't in some way point toward its key values. You cannot create in your company the landscape, music, monuments and history that call out "Duty-Honor-Country." But consider posters, signs, pictures, newsletters, songs, cards, badges, bracelets, lapel pins and other visual cues that fit your needs.

It is crucial to establish and maintain the meaning of each of these symbols. A card is just a piece of paper unless there is a clear agreement, starting at the top, throughout the organization that there is an ascribed significance. Make them worth something, by adding a cash bonus, or a ceremony. And make them more important by involving family, fellow workers, retirees or alumni. Write and choreograph your own surround system to augment and cement your culture and your leader development program.

In a large sense, the foregoing discussion about culture has been aimed at *what* it is that you wish to promote as the character component of your leadership development system. Now let's switch to *how* it is delivered, the structure.

Examine your company *structure* and improve on it.

For over two centuries West Point has refined its structure to maximize leader development. While tradition is strong, the organization, programs and processes have been tweaked and modified often to create this institution which produces leaders of character. The rank structure, the daily activities, the curriculum, the coaching program all support the goal. The four-pillar structure, cutting across academic, physical, military and character is codified and aligned to maximize success in their efforts. Cadets progress through four years of increased responsibility. Starting on day one they know they will be leaders of soldiers soon, and there are many events and challenges that convince them that they are in fact leaders already. Self-identifying as a leader is crucial.

Shifting to a typical civilian company of some size, we see a leadership development structure, as shown below. Many experts or trainers are addressing the issue at different levels.

As the chart shows, different levels of leadership receive input, coaching, and training from different organizations. Most are outside the organization but some are inside. As a general rule, the higher the leader, the more expensive the training, consulting, or coaching. The different levels are all taught leadership concepts and skills appropriate to their level of responsibilities, which makes sense. I am not recommending any change to this concept, as long as the training properly targets leadership *competencies* for the various levels.

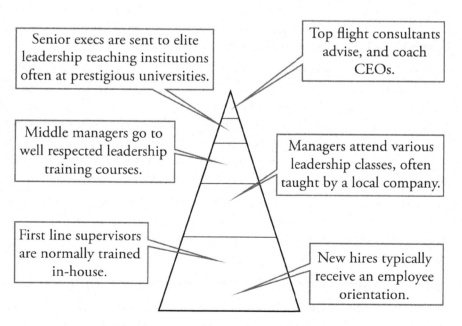

Who talks to whom about leadership?

But recall earlier in the book I distinguished between leadership character and competency:

	Character (Who you are)	Competency (What you know/do)
Definition	Principles, Values	Skills, Knowledge, Behaviors
Examples:	Respect, Honesty, Teamwork, Trust, Accountability, Integrity	Strategic Planning, Communication, Delegating Creating a vision

The different leadership (and management) training offered to different levels of the organizational pyramid are properly focused on the needs of that level or group. A senior executive needs to know how to conduct or assist in strategic planning; a first-line supervisor needs to know how to conduct a performance review. These needs at different levels are primarily in the competency domain.

From my experience, few if any of these interventions or classes offered to people at all levels deal with *character*. And a key point: character and values do not differ from the front-line supervisor to the CEO. The values are the same at all levels. If you want your total leadership team to live by the value "respect for all," that applies to the shift leader in the cafeteria as well as the COO. Similarly, one would hope that the value "integrity of reporting" applies to the line manager as well as the Chief Financial Officer.

As you develop or refine your leadership development system I suggest you retain what works from the existing multilevel training model or whatever you use, but insist leadership trainers add the character element into their programs. What do they add in terms of the character element? You have just spelled that out with your own analysis covered earlier in this chapter: the unique values and guiding behaviors for your culture are the unique character traits and guiding behaviors for leaders. These should be passed to your trainers, inside or outside the company for integration into their training. They should be pleased to do this. If they don't know how, ask them to read the next chapter.

Just as the West Point system has a four-year process, your training concept should also embody the idea that the character dimension is internalized over stages and becomes deeper and deeper with experience, coaching, and reinforcement.

A specialist in this field, Jay Conger, writes, "The best [approaches to leadership development] are designed around an understanding that leadership development is a continuous, lifelong process rather than a single event or program. They deploy more interventions—action learning, coaching, education, feedback assessments, and formal coaching…and they do so more intensely."[21]

Beyond the training template presented above, consider building in specific programs that speak to values and ethics. Recall that the cadets discussed potential ethical dilemmas with the goal that they would espouse the "right" way and verbally commit to that. Merely reading about a conundrum is only the first step. Internalizing it involves reflection, discussion, and commitment. This will steel the individual's conscience, important when the person later faces a difficult choice. Most real ethical/value challenges occur under pressure when there is no opportunity to discuss the pros and cons. Having already had that conversation with colleagues strengthens resolve.

This notion also fits the idea that character is developed by thought, dialogue, and habit. I suggest you institute structured discussions among teams of managers examining issues of conflict between values. This will cause the introspection and interactive dialogue that will cement the values and strengthen resolve.

Just like West Point, institute specific plans to focus on improving the self-image of every leader. If one of your managers thinks he is a leader, he is. So, tell your leaders they are leaders and get them up in front of a group as much as possible. Provide coaching and reinforcement. Acknowledge leaders with titles, symbols, and added recognition. Like West Point, use role models closer in age to the person being coached and equip those mentors with coaching skills.

Install your own honor system. It makes sense to think about your values as honorable ways to live and as honorable things to support and reinforce. In addition to defining the traits you value, you must also clarify what will NOT be tolerated, in terms of behaviors. Don't you want to have a "no tolerance" policy for telling racist jokes or demeaning women? Don't you want a "no tolerance" policy for any deviation from absolute integrity in financial reporting? And don't you want workable mechanisms for your leaders at all levels to correct indiscretions? That is analogous to an honor code and an honor system.

Just like the integrated four pillars of the West Point Leader Development System, your various systems need to be modified, calibrated, tweaked, and reinforced with the intent of integrating them in support of your leadership development goals.

By leader development systems, most people think first of the Human Resources Systems. And it is imperative that your recruitment, hiring, compensation, evaluation, promotion, training, and retirement systems all support your leadership development goals. For example, your interview and hiring process should be tailored to search for people who fit your leadership character goals. Similarly, your evaluation system should have a component for assessing core leadership character traits. And if character doesn't factor into your reward and promotion systems, you will join the junk pile of companies that talk a good game but don't live it.

Too often firms don't go beyond HR. I can't think of a system that shouldn't be examined and modified as needed to support leadership character development. For instance, budgeting: Does your budgeting process really support your core values of teamwork across divisions, of integrity so as not to inflate budgets or results, of accountability so that people will not search for excuses? As most of your systems are quite cyclical, set up on a fiscal year basis, and are quite complex, these system modifications may take a year or more.

In summary, if you are intent on implementing a true leader development system, you can take stock and find that you most likely have the beginnings of one already. I suggest you look at it as a complex system—a social system with input, processes, and output at multiple levels. Think of yourself as a social engineer. Pick and choose from the many ideas in this chapter. Some will fit and others will not.

It is said, "Imitation is the best form of flattery."

That suits the United States Military Academy just fine.

Chapter 9

Advice For The Leadership Instructor

**"To educate a person in mind and not in morals
is to educate a menace to society."**
Theodore Roosevelt

Memo to:

- ✓ The professor in a business school presenting a leadership program
- ✓ The teacher in a training, or consulting company offering a leadership workshop
- ✓ The instructor in a corporation training department teaching a leadership class.

From this author: "I believe I can put myself in your shoes. I have done it all my life."

On the one hand, "leadership" is a prestigious topic. It is an honor to address it in any venue. It has a ring about it. Everyone figures that if you are teaching it, you must be an expert. Often, they look up to you. They think you are a good leader. They think they want to be one. It is amazing what a positive tilt is given to "leadership" as opposed to "management." Management has a more boring, even mundane image to the layman—just doesn't have the juice. Kouzes and Posner recently observed that they never get the question, "Are managers born or made?"[1] I wonder why.

This positive view of leadership (and unflattering view of management) got a boost from scholars Zalesnik, Kotter, and Bennis several decades ago.[2] But Jay Lorsch, my professor at Harvard, objects to this "glorification of leadership," to the false dichotomy between management and leadership, and to the notion that the two are not interdependent.[3]

Regardless, the most popular authors lead this pro-leadership chorus. And I do as well.

"Leadership Training" may sound sexy, but leadership courses sometimes get poor ratings because they either restate popular principles or present obvious truisms. I painfully remember many years ago cadets referred to the course I was teaching as "leader sleep" because it lacked the challenge and rigor of other academic subjects the cadets had to face like economics or electricity.

On one occasion after I left the military, my colleague, John McKay, and I were concluding our teachings in what we felt was a very effective workshop on teamwork and leadership. We had used a lot of experiential learning, self-reflection, and sharing between colleagues to deepen and personalize topics like accountability and respect. There was some real openness and vulnerability shared among the participants which led to an increased feeling of trust and teamwork. John and I knew it had been a success. You could feel it in the room; we didn't have to wait for the "smiley sheets" for feedback.

This group was mid-level managers, each of whom was expected in about a month to assist the effort to take this workshop to his or her team, mainly salaried, blue-collar workers. We were explaining to these managers their future roles as leaders in the next workshop.

One burly supervisor in the back of the room raised his hand and challenged, "Do you really expect us to take this 'Artsy-Fartsy' stuff down to our guys on the line?"

Without a second of hesitation, as he is a lot quicker than I, John looked at me and said: "I'll be Artsy."

We laughed and then continued. And it all went well.

I tell this story because the character side of leadership doesn't lend itself to scientific inquiry, analytical precision, and intellectual reasoning. It resides in the heart. According to Dave Jolly, "The heart cannot be taught in a classroom intellectually, to students mechanically taking notes…Good, wise hearts are obtained through lifetimes of diligent effort to dig deeply within and heal lifetimes of scars…You can't teach it or email it or tweet it. It has to be discovered within the depths of one's own heart when a person is finally ready to go looking for it, and not before."[4]

When presenting values such as integrity, respect, or openness, the teacher has the challenge of talking about topics felt not thought. He or she will not really connect with the students without being very open and personally vulnerable. If the teacher is abstract and distant, the message will not sink in. If the teacher can manifest the values, in the classroom the message has a better chance of connecting.

Some instructors may have difficulty with this. It also requires a style of teaching not seen often on campuses or in company classrooms. Examine your own programs and your teaching approach as we proceed to see how you measure up, and what new ideas you could try in your unique situation.

I stated that I believe leadership is both character and competence and that character is poorly, if ever, taught. Because of that, I have focused my efforts on character rather than competency development. I will maintain that focus.

Having made the rather outlandish argument that few if any of you are doing a very good job in teaching leadership, I sincerely hope you are not offended. I am certain your students enjoyed your class and got something out of it. But did it really improve their leadership, and can you prove it?

Some highly acclaimed professors dismiss the value of classroom training:

Two Stanford professors, Jeffrey Pfeffer and Robert Sutton wrote, "… the fact is that no book, consultant, class, or series of classes, including an MBA, can teach anyone how to lead even a small team, let alone a big organization. It is a craft you can learn only through experience. This lesson about leadership is evident throughout history, and remains true despite all the training and business knowledge that has been amassed."[5]

And University of Southern California's eminent scholar and author on leadership, Warren Bennis, said, "They are not, by the way, made in a single weekend seminar, as many of the leadership-theory spokesmen claim. I've come to think of that one as the microwave theory: pop in Mr. or Ms. Average and out pops McLeader in sixty seconds."[6]

I know there are some exceptions to this rather bleak picture. One bright initiative comes recently by way of the new Chancellor of the huge University of Texas system, Admiral William McRaven. He is in the process of instituting a mandatory class on the moral, legal, and ethical aspects of leadership for its 221,000 students.[7]

Notice McRaven's focus on ethics. There are a number of courses in ethics across colleges and business schools. It is not universal, but most business schools have some form of instruction on this topic, although until recently ethics study was not even mandated for business schools by the Accreditation Council for Business Schools and Programs.[8]

I want to address ethics instruction, but first let me suggest that *ethics* is a narrower topic than *character*. While the subject of *ethics* speaks to right and wrong behavior, my notion of *character* includes other traits like respect, grit, accountability, teamwork and openness in communication—all beyond the scope of ethics.

We will return to the broader notion of character shortly; let us first examine ethics instruction.

The effectiveness of courses on ethics is questionable:

Jeffrey Seglin, an Emerson College ethics professor who writes a syndicated column on the topic, was asked if ethics can be taught, he said, "My answer is usually, 'no.' I don't think you can teach right and wrong. You can help people with ideas about how to make critical decisions."[9]

Reverend John Jenkins, president of the University of Notre Dame concurs. "It is a deep mistake to think [ethics] can be taught the way you can teach computers…Rules can be taught, but the deepest kind of ethics…requires something deeper."[10]

In a book about the Harvard Business School, Duff McDonald writes, "The question of how to incorporate ethics into the curriculum is one that dogs HBS to this day. For a variety of reasons—lack of faculty interest, lack of student interest, ongoing disagreement over how to teach it—ethics has never found true purchase at the School, amounting to nothing more than a sideshow on its best days and getting utterly ignored on its worst.[11]

The University of Chicago's Steven Kaplan asserts there is some merit to ethics courses. "To have thought about it beforehand, you are more likely to say no," he said. "If you haven't thought about it, there is some pressure to say yes."[12]

I concur. Certain choices can, and should, be predetermined. You are then better equipped when you run smack into an important decision. The good parent knows this, teaching their child what to do, for example, "…if a stranger offers to give you ride in their car…"

Similarly, thinking about future, potential ethical dilemmas can keep you out of the danger of making a wrong choice at the juncture of a temptation. It becomes more likely for your choice to be "the harder right" instead of "the easier wrong."

In an article on teaching business ethics, Jeffrey MacDonald wrote, "People who coach organizations and executives on ethics, however, say the academic approach doesn't work. Among them is John Bruhn, a Scottsdale, Arizona management consultant with an ethics specialty and an academic résumé that includes service as provost of Penn State University at Harrisburg. 'No one is going to come out of those courses as a different person … The thing those courses are going to do is create awareness. They're not going to change behavior because ethics is learned by modeling, not by reading a bunch of books over a weekend.'"[13]

MacDonald goes on to quote Marshall Goldsmith, an executive coach based in San Diego and an adjunct lecturer at Dartmouth College's Tuck School of Business. "It's unrealistic to expect people's behavior is going to change because they sit in classes …Is there any proof in any executive education … that anyone who went to any course ever changed any behavior as measured by anyone else over any period of time? Not that I know of."[14]

General Howard Prince, heading an ethics program at the University of Texas in Austin, states, "While ethics courses have a very low chance of changing people's behavior in the long run, they're still an essential starting point for laying out expectations. It's the first step. What really matters is the follow-through."[15]

I think most authorities would agree that it is rather ineffective to teach "integrity" as one would teach "finance." Traditional methods of teaching can only resort to a cognitive exercise <u>about</u> integrity. The student may well understand the importance of integrity in leadership, or perhaps the danger of diminished trust because of not having high integrity. But does the student really accept integrity to be a personal goal? This chart presents my answer:

Teaching about a trait like integrity	$\neq$	Enhancing someone's integrity

On this topic, many academics and educators use the following three all-important aspects of leadership development:`

> "*Knowing* highlights the cognitive capabilities, or the multiple intelligences, the leader requires—analytical intelligence, practical intelligence, social intelligence, emotional intelligence, and contextual intelligence are among the most commonly cited.

Doing emphasizes the behavioral or skills dimensions of becoming a leader —developing better problem solving, communication, conflict management, or adaptive skills, for example...

Being highlights that leadership is perhaps more importantly a matter of developing the identity of a leader – a self-concept that enables someone to think of himself or herself as a leader and to interact with the world from that identity or sense of being."[16]

Unfortunately, the nature of the classroom and education at large is *knowledge* focused. Your students can *know*. But can they *do*? And can they *be*? The challenge to go beyond the "know" in the typical classroom setting is your most formidable task.

My essential argument is that the development of character is not adequately covered with books and lectures. It is barely touched on in reading assignments and case studies. To understand that it is important to have *integrity* as a leader is a far cry from *deciding* to live and lead with *integrity*. Likewise, to *understand intellectually* how important it is to *respect* all people and ideas that come your way is a far cry from actually *respecting* them.

As previously quoted, Prince argues, "If one seeks only to provide learners with knowledge *about* leadership, then teaching leadership is primarily a matter of teaching in the same way one would teach any other subject in the humanities and social and behavioral sciences. One would need mainly to focus on defining a domain of knowledge and then engage the students in thinking about the subject."[17]

Prince believes that a change in one's intellectual understanding of the importance of any dimension of character is only the first step to actually committing to move in that direction. He argues to broaden it out of the classroom into student experiences elsewhere on campus and off.[18]

I want to pick up on Prince's notion to get beyond the classroom. This requires some "out-of-the-box" thinking and experimenting. To prime you for this challenge, let me describe two times in unusual places in my recent past that I have observed great creativity and results, relating to this topic. Think of them as creative exercises in the development of leadership character. These most likely won't fit for you, but they may stir your creative juices.

For my first example, meet Angie Taillon, Principal of Neil Armstrong Elementary School in Port Charlotte, Florida. Her school has a mission that resonates with several themes of this book: "To lead by example to develop character and competence in every student." Moreover, she has tabulated some 34 words she believes are important for these youngsters to understand and to live up to, including: Responsibility, Commitment, Citizenship, Positive Attitude, Adaptability, Gratitude, and Accountability. Each week one of the words is explained, and at the end of the week a student whose behavior exemplifies what the week's word means is selected in each class. Awards are periodically presented on stage at an assembly. This is for five to 10-year old's. Tell me that this is not character development.[19]

The second example I saw at the Vietnam Memorial in Washington, DC. I was visiting to honor my West Point roommate, and some other friends on "The Wall." I noticed a slew of what I presumed to be middle school kids actively searching out names of veterans killed in action. It turned out that these boys and girls were on a class trip from Ohio. They had each been given the name of a man or woman from their county back home who had died in Vietnam.

Each youngster had to go through the on-site register to determine which of many panels their soldier's name appeared on. The names are arranged chronologically by the date of death. Once a student found the name, he or she created an etching on paper to take back home. To my mind, this was a wonderful undertaking for these youngsters. It helped to personalize a connection with someone from their own world and to internalize values and character traits related to patriotism and respect for those serving our nation. Here is another school teacher thinking creatively about character instead of just being a group monitor on an field trip to the nation's capital.

I ask you to get highly creative in your own environment. Draw on some of your own experiences and background, plus the material developed in earlier chapters of this book. It has to be clear that the traditional classroom with a teacher standing up front explaining a concept like character falls woefully short.. I am going to outline for you some ideas to assist.

Let me start with what many students think of as the "end." Grading. There is such a difference between *understanding leader character* and *commitment to a principle of leadership character* that I can only think of grading the former and hoping for the latter. While I can well imagine how you could grade a student on understanding, it is not at all clear how you could grade on commitment. So, the notion of studying an author, or listening to a lecture, and then analyzing or reciting on the merits of an issue seems to fit for understanding but not for commitment. Then again, perhaps grading commitment is unnecessary.

The way to really internalize the idea of leadership character requires going beyond the normal. Some of you use leadership labs, experiential learning, written case studies, role-plays, and simulations, which offer great opportunities but have limitations. And "social learning theory" can help. This includes people observing others as role models, reflecting on experiences and case studies, and making adjustments to their character. Some of the better approaches in colleges and universities employ these methods.[20]

Others let the students explore the opposite of good character, what often is called toxic or bad leadership. This approach shows how poor leadership character can undermine the trust that is the foundation for enabling leaders to influence followers.[21]

There are great examples of teachers using dynamic case studies to understand people displaying great character. I know of at least one professor who asks his students to read John McCain's *Character is Destiny*, a series of great vignettes about very courageous people, and to come up with attributes they wish to emulate.[22] David Brooks' *The Road to Character* is another source of historic characters, each with a life-long pursuit of one character value or trait.[23] Perhaps the best known in this genre is John F. Kennedy's Pulitzer Prize winning *Profiles of Courage*.[24]

For those using these kinds of case studies on character, you may wish to consider dialogue and debate inside or out of the classroom as to how the concept might apply personally. Then fashion some mechanism for the student to report to the group on how and why this trait was picked and how and why the student plans to apply it personally. I bring this up because the social interaction, personal reflection, and vocal commitment are critical for cementing the value. It takes it from just intellectual understanding to personal ownership. That dialogue and introspection will give the concept depth and longevity for the student. Once someone has vocalized his or her own desire to behave in a given way, there is much more skin in the game to do it.

Another approach used at a lot of schools is the ethical conundrum discussion, whereby a short case study of ethical ambiguity is studied and debated. Providing a setting for students to illuminate their personal values and to listen to others' points of view can be very insightful. Often, we are faced with a difficult decision to do the "harder right rather than the easier wrong."

Debating and discussing these can be revealing and instructive. Here is an example relating to the character trait of integrity:

- ✓ You observe your manager fudging the numbers on a report to make his department look better. What do you do? Why? How?

Here is an example that spills over to teamwork:

- ✓ You have been asked by your boss to keep a business initiative secret. It has the possibility of increasing your group's headcount by three but it would eliminate 12 people from an adjacent team. You have a best friend in the other group and would like to let her know about this so she could be first in line to come to your department. What do you do? Why?

Many teachers cite newsworthy examples of ethical and character failures to discuss this topic. You don't have to look far for real and current examples of ethical and moral dilemmas to make your class relevant and timely. We can't get away from them. Normally it is well known figures who have stumbled. But I believe that is the tip of the iceberg. Thousands more cases are not news sensational because they occur lower in the organization, but they are in fact character challenges. It is probable that your students have had ample experience in this area to come up with fodder for your discussions.

Thus far in this chapter, I am sure you rightly find my suggestions to be praising current best practices.

Now comes my major recommendation which I believe to be a fresh approach—I have not seen anybody do it or suggest it.

To start with, few programs include character in their leadership programs for reasons I have discussed. Because *ethics* is often seen as a morality course, somewhat divorced from leadership, its track record is spotty and it is in many cases a hard sell. That is why I fixate on the phrase *leadership character*. It is a broader term and linked directly to the very positive topic of leadership. I am not only convinced that it is crucially needed, I believe the term is more universally accepted. Plus, leadership character includes ethics, and more.

I am bold enough to suggest that the academic leadership community pursue this venue (leadership character) rather than, or in addition to, ethics. This suggestion can be operationalized in terms of pointing doctoral candidates in this direction and repositioning and renaming the classes in the curriculum. You may argue that this is simply a semantic difference and even a marketing ploy. I am suggesting it is both.

Recent authors who have been proposing *leadership character* as an essential element of leadership are all very prescriptive. (See Chapter 4.) They wish to tell you what kind of character is going to be successful. Either from some reported research or from their own experience, they have come up with their set of values that construe how a good leader should act—as if there is one best way and one best set of values. The argument is joined for which set is best. It is an endless debate, and to my mind, futile.

I take a different tack. I believe each of us should come with a personal list of priority values. That means each student should define explicitly what aspects of this universal notion of good character seem best. There are two advantages to this approach:

- ✓ First, there will be elements of a person's character that fit the life and challenges of that person at this point in life and may not fit someone else. So, it will be much more relevant and meaningful.

- ✓ Second, when a person crafts his or her own character, ownership is sky high. And ownership, not research validity, is the core element to commitment and permanency.

My approach also defines each value or trait in a way that makes it for the individual highly specific, actionable, measurable and hence improvable. By using the trait plus guiding behaviors methodology, this topic moves from the vague to the precise, from the ether to the ground.

I am suggesting that a main part of your character program should be the requirement for your students to sketch their own desired characters in some detail and to get feedback from peers, friends, and loved ones on how they are doing and how to proceed.

They will most likely benefit from any of the case studies on character they have read or any other classroom experiences or discussions. But I am suggesting that you ask them to go through a formal process of describing their own character and getting feedback on it.

I don't use the "feedback aspect" lightly. The interaction between two people on a very deep personal topic will most likely be profound and could be life-changing for the better.

I am a disciple of the phrase "lead by example." So, my suggestion to you the professor, the consultant, or the teacher is to lead by example: Follow the protocol detailed in Chapter 4 and define your own character by developing your own *Desired Character Profile*. Then follow the protocol in Chapter 5 in experimenting with how to improve your own character. This process will give you tremendous insight into your own leadership strengths and challenges. And of paramount importance it will provide you unchallenged legitimacy with your students. Legitimacy with your students will propel them to do likewise when you adapt this for your course. You will be able to share your personal results with them. They will not only value what you have personally gained from it but also understand the process and buy into it.

Prince advises likewise: "We are continuously teaching lessons about power, interpersonal relations, communications, decision making, motivation, respect for others and much more as we interact with our students in class and elsewhere. When we practice what we teach, we not only teach, we inspire. If we ignore what we teach about leadership, we risk creating disengaged cynics."[25]

Ask the students to review the lists of character traits portrayed in Chapter 4. Show them the character traits you aspire to live up to. Continue in detail with your *Desired Character Profile* which details Guiding Behaviors for each character trait. Having demonstrated yours and from the body of work in Chapter 4, ask your students to develop their own *Desired Character Profile*. The set of character traits should be unique to each person and clearly owned by the student as well. The guiding behaviors will enhance this vague character trait with a good bit of personal definition. This should take some time.

Encourage some group dynamics within the class to allow students to express why they picked certain traits and not others. Let them share with other students some personal background that has influenced their thinking. For instance, relationship with a parent or some previous experience or one of the case studies may have had an impact. Let others provide feedback. This combination of self-reflection, open discussion and feedback from peers will cement ownership. And it will facilitate asking feedback from others not in class.

Up to this point, everything has been largely in class work with some homework. Now the real work goes on outside the class. Along the lines of what was presented in Chapter 5, students need to get feedback from others.

Returning to class and discussing the feedback will give students the opportunity to modify or calibrate their Desired Character Profile. Again, group discussions can cement the ownership going forward.

Because this is a feedback-rich process, I suggest (as discussed in Chapter 6) that you structure the class setting to include and encourage the art and practice of coaching.

The net result of this process will be that each student will come away with a very self-oriented and personal idea of what kind of character to emulate and a good deal of very useful feedback on success in the past and efforts needed for the future. The obvious, or not so obvious, intent in this suggestion is to move beyond the "understanding" of a character trait to the "commitment" to improve one's character.

This overall approach fits with what leading academics say about the process of character development, "Character is developed through a cycle of awareness, judgment, intent, behavior, and reflection."[26]

Harvard Business School's professors Khurana and Nohria suggested a Hippocratic Oath for Managers, "I pledge that considerations of personal benefit will never supersede the interests of the enterprise I am entrusted to manage. The pursuit of self-interest is the vital engine of a capitalist economy, but unbridled greed can be just as harmful. Therefore, I will guard against decisions and behavior that advance my own narrow ambitions but harm the enterprise I manage and the societies it serves."[27]

It is not a bad idea, but it has not taken flight. I think this is primarily because it is quite vague and seen as meaning little. In addition, because there are so many distinct business cultures that ask their people to abide by a certain value set, any one size does not fit all.

An institution like West Point or a corporation with a similarly well-articulated desired leadership culture has a distinct advantage over academia or training companies. The code and values for the leader development programs of these institutions are very specific and tailored. As was discussed in Chapter 7, West Point has assumed the obligation to develop leaders of character uniquely molded to their template. An institution like West Point would be the exception to the rule that each person should craft his or her own character definition.

In conclusion, your mission, should you choose it, is to revamp your curriculum using the above ideas as grist for the mill. For you, the challenge is to overcome history and the skeptics, to create and deliver an exciting and effective program, and hit this one out of the park.

That can be your legacy as a leadership teacher, mentor, and role model to future leaders.

"Leadership and learning are indispensable to each other."

From a speech John F. Kennedy was to deliver
the day he was assassinated,
November 22, 1963.[28]

Chapter 10

My Wish For You

"I am the master of my fate; I am the captain of my soul."
Invictus[1]

We have covered a lot of ground. I have asserted five major premises:

1. Leadership is not just at the top; it occurs up and down all levels of authority. And it is pervasive across industries, professions, not-for-profits, schools, sports, and government. Anywhere one person influences another, you have leadership. It is the human connection, the level of trust, the clarity of communication between the leader and the led that constitute leadership. And that influencing dynamic is personal, directional, and effective (hopefully). That is leadership at any level.

2. Leadership has two essential components:

   Competency (what you know and what you can do) Various jobs require competencies which differ markedly based not only on the level of leadership in any hierarchy, but also on the organizational demands and an infinite number of different settings. At the senior executive level, examples are creating a vision, running a board meeting, building a budget, bringing about a major change to the company. At the line manager level, examples are running a work schedule, coaching a tardy worker, enforcing safety or quality control measures, recommending a person for training.

   Character (who you are based on your values and principles) Example character traits such as integrity, openness, respect, accountability, and teamwork are necessary for good leadership across the board. These character traits are just as important as are competencies and apply universally to all levels of leadership. For instance, something like integrity is just as applicable at the bottom as it is at the top.

3. Both competency and character are essential for effective leadership. There are a host of courses and texts on improving leadership *competency*, but there are few books or programs which do justice to addressing the importance of the *character* of a leader. For this reason the focus of my effort has been on character. Character can be construed as having only a moral dimension. Who can argue with "be kind," "help an old lady cross the street," or "don't cheat on your spouse"? But when one speaks of *leadership character*, that term specifically points to character traits which encourage followership. The essential argument is: Certain character traits greatly impact the trustworthiness of the leader, and the greater the trust the greater the ability of the leader to *influence* followers. This *influence* function is the essence of leadership. Moreover, people will remember you as a leader more for who you are than what you accomplished. Character will define your real legacy as a leader.

4. If you as a leader wish to enhance this character component and to build your leadership legacy, it is important to understand that your character can and must be defined, measured, and enhanced — but only by you. All of us adults possess a fairly well-developed personality and character, but I maintain character development is a work in process. Take for instance a value often called determination, perseverance, or grit. This trait is developed early via family, friends, and school, but it can be shaped and strengthened throughout life. It is too simplistic to state that a person either has perseverance or does not. These traits are not either/or; they do not lend themselves to a binary scale. The trick is to figure out where on the scale you are for perseverance or any other value which you hold dear and which will make you a better leader. Moving up that scale is a life-long quest. Just like building your own leadership legacy is a life-long quest.

5. Easier said than done. People have been writing about and teaching values since Aristotle. I am convinced that you as a leader must define and own your personal values, those traits that make up your character or the character you wish to be. And the articulation of these values must have enough detail and specificity to make them personal and meaningful not only to you but to others. The format presented in this book, *Desired Character Profile,* lends itself to that end. Moreover this is a vehicle that can solicit feedback from friends and colleagues, prompt commitment on your part to improve, and enable repeated

measurement over time. Essentially my recommendation is a process of personally defining your character, getting feedback from others, seriously reflecting on it, and committing to what you wish to change. This fundamental methodology is applicable to those executives who wish to create leadership development systems in their corporations as well as to teachers of the subject of leadership from company classrooms to MBA programs.

Now comes the real test of how effective I have been—and how much you care about building your leadership legacy.

Character enhancement does not come from a book, even this book. You may get some cognitive sense of how important integrity is for you as a leader by reading a text or case study. But most likely you will not modify your character or behavior just by knowing how important (on an intellectual level) it is. An obvious example is the fact that few of us always eat what we know is the healthiest choice.

Here is another example from one of my favorite character traits, "openness." This could encompass being *open* to feedback, to new ideas, to new ways of doing things, to input from any source, or even to being wrong. It could also mean being *open* in communicating to others, telling it honestly, speaking truth to power, keeping others informed. The vast majority of followers would like their leader to have this trait, for sure.

Leaders can be taught communication skills galore with the result that they *know* how important openness is. Knowing to be open is important but insufficient. To really make a change, to actually "move the needle" on your character, requires for you to own it, for you to reflect on it, for you to define it, for you to assess it, for you to get feedback on it, and for you to commit to improving it. This process is time-consuming and not easy to do in a classroom setting. It is developed over time with a conscious application of self-reflection, communication with peers and friends, and commitment to make a difference.

So the real test of my effectiveness as an author is whether or not you will own and run with any of the ideas suggested herein. And if it all makes perfect intellectual sense, but you opt to do nothing, then you fit the mold of this wonderful Chinese proverb.

"To know, but not to do, is not yet to know."

Wang Yangming (1472-1529)[2]

119

And if you then say that you will "try" to do some of the suggestions enumerated in this book, you need to listen to the wisdom of Yoda:

"Try? There is no try. There is only do or do not do."

Yoda, "The Empire Strikes Back"³

If on the other hand, you want to make something happen, my wish for you is that:

- This focus on character changes your approach to leadership in a transformational way.

- It impacts you personally and, through you, those with whom you interact, coach or teach.

- This will produce a geometric improvement in your leadership and in the leadership of everyone with whom you come into contact.

Good luck and best wishes.

Notes

Preface

1. D. Brooks. *The Road to Character.* New York: Random House, 2015. p. xi.

Chapter 1

1. This paraphrases US Supreme Court Justice Potter Stewart in a 1964 case about obscenity.

2. B. Kellerman. *The End of Leadership.* New York: HarperCollins, 2012.

3. There are scores of biographies of Ike. To learn how he developed his own leadership as a young man, well before he wore stars, read: R. Carroll, "The Making of a Leader: Dwight D, Eisenhower." *Military Review,* January- February 2009.

4. D. Castello "There's Nothing Wrong With Our Radar!" *Castello Cities Internet Network, Inc.* Pearl Harbor.com 2001-2017. Accessed March 20, 2017 on www.pearl-harbor.com/georgeelliott

5. J. French and B. Raven. "The Bases of Social Power." *Studies in Social Power,* Dorwin Cartwright (ed.), Research Center for Group Dynamics, Institute for Social Research, University of Michigan, Ann Arbor: 1959. pp. 150-167.

6. A. Tennyson. "The Charge of the Light Brigade." As accessed on June 4, 2017 at www.poetry.eserver.org/light-brigade.html

Chapter 2

1. W. Bennis. "Leadership Theory and Administrative Behavior: The Problem with Authority." *Administrative Science Quarterly*, 1959. p.259.

2. M. Weber. *The Protestant Ethic and the Spirit of Capitalism.* New York: Routledge Classics, 1930.

3. F. Taylor. *The Principles of Scientific Management.* New York: Harper and Brothers, 1911.

4. E. Mayo. *The Human Problems of an Industrial Civilization.* New York: Viking Press, 1960.

5. P. Drucker. *The Practice of Management.* New York: HarperCollins, 1990.

6. A. Maslow. *Motivation and Personality.* New York: Harper and Brothers, 1954.

7. F. Stogdill. *Handbook of leadership: A survey of theory and research.* New York, NY, US: Free Press, 1974. The Ohio studies spawned two other great luminaries in the field of leadership, Bernard Bass and Bruce Avolio.

8. J. Burns, *Leadership.* New York: Harper and Row, 1978.

9. W. Deming. *Quality, Productivity, and Competitive Position.* Cambridge MA: Massachusetts Institute of Technology, Center for Advanced Engineering Study, 1982. pp 16-55.

10. J. Gardner. *On Leadership.* New York: The Free Press, 1993.

11. T. Peters and R. Waterman. *In Search of Excellence.* New York: Harper and Row, 1982.
W. Bennis and B. Nanus. *Leaders: Strategies for Taking Charge.* New York: Harper & Row, 1985.
W. Bennis. *On Becoming a Leader.* New York: Random House Business Books, 1989.
J. Kotter. *A Force for Change, How Leadership Differs from Management.* New York: The Free Press, 1990.
J. Kotter. *Leading Change.* Boston MA: Harvard Business School Press, 1996.
J. Kotter. *John P. Kotter on What Leaders Really Do.* Boston MA: Harvard Business School Press, 1999.
J. Kotter and D. Cohen. *The Heart of Change, Real-Life Stories About How People Change Their Organizations.* Boston MA: Harvard Business School Press, 2002.

12. D. Carnegie. *How to Win Friends and Influence Enemies.* New York: Simon & Schuster, 1936.

13. S. Covey. *The 7 Habits of Highly Effective People. New York:* Simon & Shuster, 1989.

14. W. Ulmer. "Toxic Leadership, What Are We Talking About." *Army Magazine,* June 2012. p. 48.

15. R. Hogan and J. Hogan. "Assessing Leadership: A View from the Dark Side." *International Journal of Selection and Assessment,* March/June 2001.

16. D. McDonald. *The Golden Passport, Harvard Business School, the limits of capitalism, and the moral failure or the MBA elite.* New York: Harper Collins, 2017. p. 313.

17. J. Pfeffer, as quoted in Andrews, M. "Teaching leadership for change in the business school." *University World News,* May 27, 2016. Accessed on March 30, 2017. www.universityworldnews.com

18. https://en.wikipedia.org/wiki/Master_of_Business_Administration#History

19. https://www.ed.gov/ https://en.wikipedia.org/wiki/List_of_business_schools_in_the_United_States;

20. https://www.hbs.edu/

21. https://www.ccl.org/

22. D. McDonald. *The Golden Passport, Harvard Business School, the limits of capitalism, and the moral failure or the MBA elite.* New York: Harper Collins, 2017. p. 159.

23. S. Adams. "The Most Prestigious Consulting Firms In 2015." Forbes: accessed March 22, 2017 at www.forbes.com/sites/susanadams

24. PricewaterhouseCoopers website accessed Mar 22, 2017: www.pwc.com

25. J. Conger presents an overview of the field of experiential courses in *Learning to Lead, the Art of Transforming Managers into Leaders.* San Francisco: Jossey-Bass Publishers, 1992.

26. American Management Association web site accessed March 22, 2017: www.amanet.org

27. J. Zenger. "We Wait Too Long to Train Our Leaders." *Harvard Business Review.* Dec 17, 2012.

28. M. Andrews. "Teaching Leadership for Change in the Business School." *University World News.* 27 May 2016. Accessed March 22, 2017: www.universityworldnews.com

29. Ibid.

30. H. Prince. "Teaching Leadership: A Journey Into The Unknown." Concepts and Connections: A Newsletter for Leadership Educators. Vol. 9, 2001.

31. B. Kellerman. *The End of Leadership*. New York: HarperCollins, 2012. pp xxiv-xxv.

32. J. Van Maanen. As quoted by Duff McDonald in "Can You Learn to Lead" in the New York Times and accessed July 9, 2017. https://www.nytimes.com/2015/04/12/education/edlife/12edl-12leadership.html

33. J. Pfeffer. *Leadership BS: Fixing Workplaces and Careers One Truth at a Time*. New York: HarperCollins, 2015.

34. J. Pfeffer and R. Sutton. *Hard Facts, Dangerous Half-Truths And Total Nonsense: Profiting From Evidence-Based Management*. Boston, MA: 2006.

35. N. Nohria and R. Khurana. *Handbook of Leadership Theory and Practice, A Harvard Business School Centennial Colloquium*. Boston: Harvard Business School Press, 2010. p. 5.

36. W. Deresiewicz. *Excellent Sheep the Miseducation of the American Elite and the Way to a Meaningful Life*. NY: Free Press, 2014.

37. A. Lytle, professor and director of leadership at Monash Business School in Australia as quoted by M. Andrews. "Teaching Leadership for Change in the Business School." *University World News*. 27 May 2016. Accessed March 22, 2017: www.universityworldnews.com

38. S. Datar, D. Garvin and P. Cullen. *Rethinking the MBA: Business Education at a Crossroads*. Boston: Harvard Business Press, 2010.

Chapter 3

1. L. Dhir, Associate Professor at the SP Jain Institute of Management and Research, India, as quoted by Margaret Andrews, "Teaching Leadership for Change in the Business School." 27 May 2016 University World News www.universityworldnews.com

2. I notice that fellow West Point graduate Dave Anderson and I have used a similar teaching technique as he describes in the excellent book he and his father wrote, *Becoming a Leader of Character*, New York: Morgan James, 2017. He similarly referred to Generals Palmer and Schwarzkopf as do I in my book. I guarantee I did not copy him. I did pick up from his text a lot of excellent general quotations on the topic of character.

3. J. Kotter. *Leading Change*. Boston MA: Harvard Business School Press, 1996.

4. J. Kotter, J. and D. Cohen. *The Heart of Change, Real-Life Stories About How People Change Their Organizations*. Boston MA: Harvard Business School Press, 2002.

5. W. Bennis. *On Becoming a Leader*. New York: Random House Business Books, 1989.

6. C. Dweck. "Student Motivation: What Works, What Doesn't," *Education Week*, Aug 30, 2006.

7. A. Duckworth. *Grit: The Power of Passion and Perseverance*. New York: Simon & Schuster, 2016.

8. C. D'Este. *Patton, A Genius for War*. New York: HarperCollins, 1995.

9. R. Sturma, D. Vera, and M. Crossan. "The entanglement of leader character and leader competence and its impact on performance." *The Leadership Quarterly*. 28 (2017). p. 350.

10. Ibid. p. 349.

11. J. Pfeffer and R. Sutton. *Hard Facts, Dangerous Half-Truths and Total Nonsense*. Boston: Harvard Business Review Press, 2006.

12. D. Barton, head of McKinsey's global consulting practice; commencement address MBA convocation, Ivey Business School, Western University, London Canada, delivered June 6 2014, as quoted in Crossan, M., G. Seijts, and J. Gandz. *Developing Leadership Character*. New York: Taylor &Francis, 2016. pp. 2,3.

Chapter 4

1. "Strong's Concordance 5481" *NAS Exhaustive Concordance of the Bible with Hebrew-Aramaic and Greek Dictionaries*, The Lockman Foundation, 1998.

2. W. Fung, Managing Director, Li & Fung Group, (global trading company) Hong Kong

3. S. O'Brien, TV anchor and CEO of Starfish Media Group, a multi-platform media production company as quoted by Adam Bryant in "Corner Office", *New York Times*. June 12, 2016.

4. T. Lewis, Chief of Police Punta Gorda, Florida as quoted in *The Englewood Sun*, Nov 6, 2016.

5. S. Reynolds, ed., *Thoughts of Chairman Buffett: Thirty years of Unconventional Wisdom from the Sage of Omaha.* New York: Harper Business, 2011. p. 64.

6. D. Brooks. *The Road to Character.* New York: Random House, 2015. p. 253.

7. R. Reeves. "The New Politics of Character" *National Affairs* Number 20 – Summer 2014.

8. B. Avolio. "Pursuing Authentic Leadership Development." *Handbook of Leadership Theory and Practice; a Harvard Business School Centennial Colloquium.* Boston: Harvard Business School Press, 2010. p. 756.

9. Marcus Tullius Cicero (106–43 B.C.), *Internet Encyclopedia of Philosophy*, accessed on Mar 30, 2017: *www.iep.utm.edu/cicero/*

10. G. Chesterton. *Quotations of G. K. Chesterton - American Chesterton Society* accessed at *https://www.chesterton.org/quotations-of-g-k-chesterton/*

11. W. Shakespeare. "All's Well that Ends Well" act 3 scene 5.

12. C. Shields. "Aristotle's Philosophical Life and Writings." *The Oxford Handbook of Aristotle.* New York: Oxford University Press, 2012.

13. M. Crossan, G. Seijts, and J. Gandz. *Developing Leadership Character.* New York: Taylor &Francis, 2016. pp 1-13.

14. T. Clark. *Leading with Character & Competence.* Oakland CA: Berrett-Koehler, 2016. pp 17-86.

15. R. Riggio, W. Zhu, C. Reina, and J. Maroosis. "VIRTUE-BASED MEASUREMENT OF ETHICAL LEADERSHIP: THE LEADERSHIP VIRTUES QUESTIONNAIRE" *Psychology Journal: Practice and Research.* American Psychological Association, December 2010. Vol. 62, No. 4, 235-250.

16. M. Grahek, A. Thompson, and A. Toliver. "THE CHARACTER TO LEAD: A CLOSER LOOK AT CHARACTER IN LEADERSHIP." *Psychology Journal: Practice and Research.* American Psychological Association, December 2010. Vol. 62, No. 4, 270-290.

17. R. Reeves. Op cit.

18. VIA, Values in Action, accessed on March 30, 2017 at http://www.viacharacter.org/www/

19. J. Anderson, J.L. and D. Anderson D. *Becoming a Leader of Character*, New York: Morgan James, 2017. p. 41.

20. Heraclitus (Greek Philosopher 540 BC - 480 BC), from Discourse "On the Universe"; within "On Nature" accessed Mar 25, 2017 at: en.wikipedia.org/wiki/On Nature_(Heraclitus)

Chapter 5

1. J. Froude. (1818 - 1894) Oxford lecturer.

2. OCEAN Model instrument, NEO-IPIP accessed at http://www.personalitytest.net/ipip/ipipneo120.html

3. R. Hughes, R. Ginnett, and G. Curphy. *Leadership, Enhancing the Lessons of Experience*. NY: McGraw-Hill, 2016. p. 197.

4. R. Kegan and L. Lahey "Adult Development and Organizational Leadership." *Handbook of Leadership Theory and Practice, A Harvard Business School Centennial Colloquium*. Boston: Harvard Business School Press, 2010. p. 786.

5. B. Avolio. "Pursuing Authentic Leadership Development." *Handbook of Leadership Theory and Practice; a Harvard Business School Centennial Colloquium*. Boston: Harvard Business School Press, 2010. p. 740.

6. Ibid. p. 755.

7. C. McCauley and E. Van Velsor (editors) *The Center for Creative Leadership Handbook of Leadership Development 2d edition*. San Francisco: Jossey-Bass, 2004.

8. C. McCauley and C. Douglas. "Developmental Relationships." *The Center for Creative Leadership Handbook of Leadership Development 2d edition*. San Francisco: Jossey-Bass, 2004.

9. R. Carroll "The Making of a Leader: Dwight D, Eisenhower." *Military Review*, January- February 2009.

10. J. Haidt. "The Moral Roots of Liberals and Conservatives." *Tedtalks*. Mar 2008 accessed March 28 2017 on www.ted.com/talks/jonathan_haidt_on_the_moral_mind?language=en

11. J. Lorsch. "A Contingency Theory of Leadership." *Handbook of Leadership Theory and Practice, A Harvard Business School Centennial Colloquium*. Boston: Harvard Business School Press, 2010.

12. R. Kegan and L. Lahey "Adult Development and Organizational Leadership." *Handbook of Leadership Theory and Practice, A Harvard Business School Centennial Colloquium.* Boston: Harvard Business School Press, 2010.

13. E. Van Velsor and W. Drath. "A Lifelong Developmental Perspective on Leader Development." *The Center for Creative Leadership Handbook of Leadership Development 2d edition.* San Francisco: Jossey-Bass, 2004.

14. Op. Cit. McCauley and Van Velsor. p. 3.

15. H. Levinson as quoted in McDonald, D. *The Golden Passport, Harvard Business School, the limits of capitalism, and the moral failure or the MBA elite.* New York: Harper Collins, 2017. Pp. 150-151.

16. I. B. Myers. *Introduction to Type: A Description of the Theory and Applications of the Myers-Briggs Type Indicator* Palo Alto, CA: Consulting Psychologists Press, 1987.

17. On line character surveys:
www.viacharacter.org/viainstitute/classification.aspx
www.kconnection.com/character+competence-sa
www.sigmaassessmentsystems.com
www.andersonleadershipsolutions.com/character-test/

18. On line games to assess character and other elements for recruiting purposes:
www.stockfuse.com
www.nack.it.com
www.pymetrics.com
www.tycoonsystems.com

19. W. Bennis. *On Becoming a Leader.* NY: Random House Business Books, 1989.

Chapter 6

1. M. Follett. *The Creative Experience.* New York: Longmans, Green, 1924.

2. www.en.wikipedia.org/wiki/McDonald's

3. C. McCauley and E. Van Velsor (editors) *The Center for Creative Leadership: Handbook of Leadership Development 2d edition.* San Francisco: Jossey-Bass, 2004.

4. E. Van Velsor, R. Moxley, and K. Bunker. "The Leader Development Process." *The Center for Creative Leadership: Handbook of Leadership Development 2d edition.* San Francisco: Jossey-Bass, 2004. p. 205.

5. Authenticity in question. Not sure a scribe on the Mongolian Steppes in 1206 AD would have captured such an eloquent quote, much less passed it on to the English speaking world.

6. R. Likert. *The Human Organization: Its Management and Value.* New York: McGraw-Hill, 1967.

7. E. Burritt. 17th Century American Diplomat and Social Activist

Chapter 7

1. R. Caslen, Lieutenant General, Superintendent. *West Point.* A Publication of the West Point Association of Graduates. West Point NY, Spring 2017. p. 4.

2. D. Eisenhower letter to Maxwell Taylor Jan 2, 1946. West Point Library Archives, West Point, NY.

3. E. Barrett. "The Four Pillars of the West Point Leader Development System." *West Point.* A Publication of the West Point Association of Graduates. West Point NY, Winter 2017. p 15.

4. Ibid.

5. K. Hamel. "USMA's Academic Program." *West Point.* A Publication of the West Point Association of Graduates. West Point NY, Winter 2017. pp 16-20.

6. K. Hamel. "USMA's Military Program." *West Point.* A Publication of the West Point Association of Graduates. West Point NY, Winter 2017. pp 22-29.

7. K. Hamel. "USMA's Physical Program." *West Point.* A Publication of the West Point Association of Graduates. West Point NY, Winter 2017. pp 30-37.

8. Dengfeng Zhen, Member of the Chinese Communist Party, in a conversation in Beijing, following his visit to West Point, 2015.

9. *Bugle Notes '58.* West Point annual publication. West Point NY: United States Military Academy, 1958.

10. J. Collins. "Foreword" *Leadership Lessons from West Point, (Crandall editor),* San Francisco: Wiley, 2006.

11. H. Ibarra, S. Snook, and L.G. Ramo. "Identity-Based Leader Development." *Handbook of Leadership Theory and Practice, A Harvard Business School Centennial Colloquium.* Boston: Harvard Business School Press, 2010. pp. 658.

12. S. Ambrose. *Duty, Honor, Country, A History of West Point.* Baltimore MD: Johns Hopkins University Press, 1996. pp. 278, 279.

13. *Bugle Notes.* West Point annual publication. West Point NY: United States Military Academy, years 1950-1988.

14. Ibid. years 1989-2016.

15. Op. cit. Barrett. p. 15.

16. N. Nohria and R. Khurana. *Handbook of Leadership Theory and Practice, A Harvard Business School Centennial Colloquium.* Boston: Harvard Business School Press, 2010. p. 4.

17. B. Kellerman. *The End of Leadership.* New York: HarperBusiness, 2012. p 156

18. S. Datar, D. Garvin and P. Cullen. *Rethinking the MBA: Business Education at a Crossroads.* Boston: Harvard Business Press, 2010.

19. K. Hamel. "Every Graduate a Leader of Character." *West Point.* A Publication of the West Point Association of Graduates. West Point NY, Winter 2017. P. 40.

20. Ibid.

21. West Point Pamphlet. *West Point Leader Development System.* West Point NY: United States Military Academy, 2015. p.5.

22. West Point Pamphlet "Building Capacity to Lead." West Point NY: United States Military Academy, 2009. p. 18.

23. E. Goffman. *Asylums: Essays on the Social Situation of Mental Patients and Other Inmates.* New York: Random House, 1961.

24. Op. Cit. Ambrose. pp. 278, 279.

25. West Point Course Syllabus, MX 400 Officership. West Point NY: United States Military Academy, 2017. p.4.

26. Op. Cit. Ambrose. p. x.

27. "What Price Honor? The West Point Scandal." *Time Magazine.* June 7, 1976.

28. Presentation. "Academic Ethics." The Center for Academic Integrity, the LBJ School of Public Policy, June 2005.

29. D. Callahan. "Cheating Culture." *Plagiary: cross-disciplinary studies in plagiarism, fabrication, and falsification.* Ann Arbor, MI: Scholarly Publications Office, University of Michigan Library, 2006. pp. 26, 29.

30. M. McDonald. "Dartmouth Gives Students a Lesson: Don't Cheat in Ethics Class." *Bloomberg Business.* Jan 8, 2015.

31. D. McCabe. As reported by M. Keenan and B. Sullivan. "Duke Probe Shows Failure of Post-Enron Ethics Classes." *Bloomberg Business.* May 2007.

32. D. McDonald. *The Golden Passport, Harvard Business School, the limits of capitalism, and the moral failure or the MBA elite.* New York: Harper Collins, 2017.

33. A. Novotney. "Beat the Cheat." American Psychology Association June 2001, Vol 42, No. 6. p .54.

34. Op. Cit. *Bugle Notes '58.*

35. R. Carroll. "Ethics of the Military Profession." *Air University Review,* November-December 1974. pp 40-43.

36. "Leader Challenge: Company Command, Building Combat-Ready Teams." *Army Magazine.* June 2013.

37. Op. cit. Barrett. p. 41.

38. West Point Course Syllabus, MX 400 Officership. West Point NY: United States Military Academy, 2017.

39. West Point Pamphlet. *USCC Pamphlet 15-1. The Cadet Honor Code, System, and Committee Procedures.* West Point NY: Headquarters United States Corps of Cadets, 9 October 2015.

40. Op. Cit. *Bugle Notes '58.*

41. Op. Cit. *Bugle Notes '58.*

Chapter 8

1. E. Webb, Lieutenant Colonel, US Army, Infantry Battalion Commander, the Federal Republic of Germany. Best I ever saw. Not a verbatim quote, but I bet he said something close to this. 1977.

2. P. Donahue, CEO of McDonald's of Canada during several conversations in 2000 and since.

3. R. Carroll "Three Simple Rules of Leadership, Dream it. Define it. Do it!" *Journal of Quality and Participation*, July/August 1992.

4. E. Schein with P. Schein. *Organizational Culture and Leadership 5th Edition*. Hoboken NJ: John Wiley &Sons. 2017. P. 6. (editions: 1985, 1992, 2004, 2010)

5. J. Van Maanen. and E. Schein "Toward a Theory of Organizational Socialization." *Research in Organizational Behavior*. Vol 1. Greenwich CT: JAI Press, 1979.

6. H. Becker. *Outsiders*. New York: Simon & Schuster, 1963.

7. J. Kotter and J. Haskett in *Corporate Culture and Performance*. New York: Simon & Schuster, 1992, point to Andrew Pettigrew's "On Studying Organizational /Culture," *Administrative Science Quarterly*. *24*. 1979 as the "first scholarly work to focus on organizational culture." E. Schein dates 1978 as the year that roles, norms, and values were identified as the components of organizational culture, as outlined in D. Katz and R. Kahn. *The Social Psychology of Organizations*. New York: John Wiley and Sons, 1978.

8. T. Deal and A. Kennedy. *Corporate Cultures: The Rites and Rituals of Corporate Life*. NY: HarperCollins, 1982.

9. L. Senn and J. Childress. *The Secret of a Winning Culture*. Los Angeles, CA: Leadership Press, 1999. I credit Senn Delaney Leadership Consulting Group with the terminology, techniques and methodology for examining the culture of a company. Much of what I present in this chapter was learned from great teachers in that company.

10. J. Kotter and J. Haskett. *Corporate Culture and Performance*. New York: Simon & Schuster, 1992. p. 11.

11. Ibid. p 78

12. Op. Cit. Senn and Kotter. I use Senn-Delaney's terms to describe a company's culture, namely "Values" and "Guiding Behaviors." Kotter and Haskett used similar terms, "Core Values" and "Common Behaviors."

13. Op. Cit. Senn.

14. Ibid.

15. P. Lencioni. "Make Your Values Mean Something." *Harvard Business Review.* Boston: July 2002. p. 113

16. Ibid.

17. http://www.alibabagroup.com/en/about/culture

18. J. Conger. "Leadership Development Interventions." *Handbook of Leadership Theory and Practice, A Harvard Business School Centennial Colloquium.* Boston: Harvard Business School Press, 2010. p. 720. IBM's Gerstner simplified a set of eleven competencies (customer insight, breakthrough thinking, drive to achieve, team leadership, straight talk, teamwork, decisiveness, building organizational capability, coaching, personal dedication, passion for the business), which he felt caused a lack of focus.

19. L. Long. Principal of Charlotte High School. "Pirates lead, others follow" as quoted in *The Englewood (FL) Sun,* Jan 29, 2016.

20. http://www.mars.com/global/about-us/history

21. Op. Cit. Conger. p. 713.

Chapter 9

1. J. Kouzes. and B. Posner. *Learning Leadership, the Five Fundamentals of Becoming an Exemplary Leader.* San Francisco: The Leadership Challenge, A Wiley Brand, 2016. p. 3.

2. A. Zalesnik. "Managers and Leaders: Are They Different?" *Harvard Business Review*, 1977.
   W. Bennis. *On Becoming a Leader.* New York: Random House Business Books, 1989.
   J. Kotter. *Leading Change.* Boston: Harvard Business School Press, 1996.

3. J. Lorsch. "A Contingency Theory of Leadership." *Handbook of Leadership Theory and Practice; a Harvard Business School Centennial Colloquium.* Boston: Harvard Business School Press, 2010. pp. 411-413.

4. D. Jolly as quoted by D. Brooks. *The Road to Character.* New York: Random House, 2015. p. xv.

5. J. Pfeffer and R. Sutton. *Hard Facts, Dangerous Half-Truths and Total Nonsense.* Boston: Harvard Business Review Press, 2006. as quoted by M. McCall in "The Experience Conundrum." *Handbook of Leadership Theory and Practice; a Harvard Business School Centennial Colloquium.* Boston: Harvard Business School Press, 2010. p. 679.

6. W. Bennis. *On Becoming a Leader.* New York: Random House Business Books, 1989. p. 42.

7. W. McRaven, Admiral US Navy (Retired), <u>Chancellor</u> of the <u>University of Texas System</u>. *Fox News With Chris Wallace.* April 9, 2017.

8. Accreditation Council for Business Schools and Programs at http://www.acbsp.org/

9. J. Seglin as quoted by J. Cohen and G. Burns. "Can you teach a person ethics?" *Chicago Tribune.* June 7, 2006.

10. J. Jenkins. as quoted by J. Cohen and G. Burns. "Can you teach a person ethics?" *Chicago Tribune.* June 7, 2006.

11. D. McDonald. *The Golden Passport, Harvard Business School, the limits of capitalism, and the moral failure or the MBA elite.* New York: Harper Collins, 2017. p 94.

12. S. Kaplan. as quoted by J. Cohen and G. Burns. "Can you teach a person ethics?" *Chicago Tribune.* June 7, 2006.

13. G. MacDonald. "Can business ethics be taught?" *The Christian Science Monitor,* 2007.

14. Ibid.

15. H. Prince. as quoted by J. Cohen and G. Burns. "Can you teach a person ethics?" *Chicago Tribune.* June 7, 2006.

16. N. Nohria and R. Khurana. "Advancing Leadership Theory and Practice." *Handbook of Leadership Theory and Practice, A Harvard Business School Centennial Colloquium.* Boston: Harvard Business School Press, 2010. p 21.

17. H. Prince. "Teaching Leadership: A Journey Into The Unknown." *Concepts and Connections: A Newsletter for Leadership Educators,* Vol. 9 (3); 1, 3, 13; 2001.

18. Ibid.

19. A. Taillon, Principal of Neil Armstrong Elementary School, Port Charlotte FL as reported in OP ED "Developing character … in youth" *Englewood Sun*, January 27, 2017.

20. C. McCauley and C. Douglas. "Developmental Relationships" *The Center for Creative Leadership Handbook of Leadership Development 2d edition*. San Francisco: Jossey-Bass, 2004.

21. R. Hogan and J. Hogan. "Assessing Leadership: A View from the Dark Side." *International Journal of Selection and Assessment*, March/June 2001.
Ulmer W. "Toxic Leadership, What Are We Talking About." *Army Magazine*, June 2012.
B. Kellerman. *Bad Leadership: What It Is, How It Happens, Why It Matters*. Boston MA: Harvard Business School Press, 2004.

22. J. McCain with M. Salter. *Character is Destiny.* New York: Random House, 2005.

23. D. Brooks. *The Road to Character.* New York: Random House, 2015.

24. J. Kennedy. *Profiles in Courage.* New York: Harper and Brothers, 1956.

25. H. Prince. op cit.

26. Sturm, R., D. Vera, and M. Crossan. "The entanglement of leader character and leader competence and its impact on performance." *The Leadership Quarterly.* 28 (2017). p. 351.

27. R. Khurana and N. Nohria. "It's Time to Make Management a True Profession" *Harvard Business Review*. Boston: Oct 2008.

28. J. Hickman. "Leaders Making Leaders: Crafting Effective Learning Strategies to Promote Army Leadership." Center For Faculty Excellence, West Point NY: United States Military Academy, 2016.

Chapter 10

1. W.E. Henley. Poem *"Invictus."* (Latin for unconquered) *A Book of Verses*. London: Scribner & Welford, 1891.

2. www.azquotes.com/author/19984-Wang_Yangming

3. Video. "Star Wars: The Empire Strikes Back." 1980.

Bibliography

"Academic Ethics." Presentation by The Center for Academic Integrity, the LBJ School of Public Policy, June 2005.

Accreditation Council for Business Schools and Programs at http://www.acbsp.org/

Adams, S. "The Most Prestigious Consulting Firms In 2015." *Forbes*: accessed March 22, 2017 at www.forbes.com/sites/susanadams

Ambrose, S. *Duty, Honor, Country, A History of West Point.* Baltimore MD: Johns Hopkins University Press, 1996.

American Management Association web site accessed March 22, 2017: www.amanet.org

Anderson, J. and D. Anderson. *Becoming a Leader of Character*, New York: Morgan James, 2017.

Andrews, M. "Teaching leadership for change in the business school." *University World News,* May 27, 2016. Accessed on March 30, 2017. www.universityworldnews.com

Avolio, B. "Pursuing Authentic Leadership Development." *Handbook of Leadership Theory and Practice; a Harvard Business School Centennial Colloquium.* Boston: Harvard Business School Press, 2010.

Avolio, B. and W. Gardner, "Authentic Leadership Development: Getting to the Root of Positive Forms of Leadership." *Leadership Quarterly* 16. 2005.

Barnard, C. *The Functions of the Executive, 1938.* Cambridge, MA: Harvard University Press, 1968.

Barrett, E. "The Four Pillars of the West Point Leader Development System. *"West Point.* A Publication of the West Point Association of Graduates. West Point NY, Winter 2017.

Barton, D., Head of McKinsey's Global Consulting Practice in commencement address at the MBA Convocation, Ivey Business School, Western University, London, Ontario, Canada, June 6, 2014. As quoted in *Developing Leadership Character.* New York: Taylor & Francis, 2016.

Bass, B. and P. Steidlmeier, "Ethics, character, and authentic transformational leadership behavior." *Leadership Quarterly*, 10 (2), 181-217, 1999.

Becker, H. *Outsiders.* New York: Simon & Schuster, 1963.

Beckhard, R. and W. Pritchard. *Changing the Essence, The Art of Creating and Leading Fundamental Change in Organizations.* San Francisco: Josses-Bass Inc. 1992.

Bennis W. *On Becoming a Leader.* New York: Random House Business Books, 1989.

Bennis W. and B. Nanus, *Leaders: Strategies for Taking Charge.* New York: Harper & Row, 1985.

Bennis, W. "Leadership Theory and Administrative Behavior: The Problem with Authority." *Administrative Science Quarterly*, 1959.

Berger, L. and D. Berger. *The Talent Management Handbook: Creating Organizational Excellence by Identifying, Developing, and Promoting Your Best People.* New York: McGraw Hill, 2004.

Betros, L. (2012). *Carved from granite: West Point since 1902.* [Kindle Edition]. Retrieved from http://www.amazon.com

Brooks, D. *The Road to Character.* New York: Random House, 2015.

Bryant, A. "Corner Office", *New York Times*. June 12, 2016.

Burns, J. *Leadership.* New York: Harper & Row, 1978.

Byham, W. et al *Grow Your Own Leaders: How to Identify, Develop, and Retain Leadership Talent.* Upper Saddle River, NJ: Prentice Hall, 2002.

Callahan, D. "Cheating Culture." *Plagiary: cross-disciplinary studies in plagiarism, fabrication, and falsification.* Ann Arbor, MI: Scholarly Publications Office, University of Michigan Library, 2006.

Carnegie, D. *How to Win Friends and Influence Enemies.* New York: Simon & Schuster, 1936.

Carroll, R. "Ethics of the Military Profession." *Air University Review*, November-December 1974.

Carroll, R. "The Making of a Leader: Dwight D, Eisenhower." *Military Review*, January–February 2009.

Carroll, R. "Three Simple Rules of Leadership, Dream it. Define it. Do it!" *Journal of Quality and Participation*, July/August 1992.

Carter, L., D. Giber, and M. Goldsmith (editors) *Linkage Inc.'s Best Practices in Organization Development and Change: Culture, Leadership, Retention, Performance, Coaching* San Francisco: Jossey-Bass, 2001.

Caslen, R., Lieutenant General, Superintendent. *West Point.* A Publication of the West Point Association of Graduates. West Point NY, Spring, 2017.

Castello, D. "There's Nothing Wrong With Our Radar!" *Castello Cities Internet Network, Inc.* Pearl Harbor.com 2001-2017. Accessed March 20, 2017.

Chesterton, G. *Quotations of G. K. Chesterton—American Chesterton Society https://www.chesterton.org/quotations-of-g-k-chesterton/*

Childress, J. *A Time for Leadership.* Long Beach CA: The Leadership Press, Inc, 2000.

Childress, J. and L. Senn. *In the Eye of the Storm, Reengineering Corporate Culture,* Long Beach CA: The Leadership Press, Inc, 1995.

Cialdini, R. *Influence: The Psychology of Persuasion* and *Influence.* New York: William Morrow and Co, 1984.

Cicero, Marcus Tullius (106–43 B.C.), *Internet Encyclopedia of Philosophy,* accessed on Mar 30, 2017: www.iep.utm.edu/cicero/

Clark, T. *Leading with Character & Competence.* Oakland CA: Berrett-Koehler, 2016.

Cohen, J. and G. Burns. "Can you teach a person ethics?" *Chicago Tribune.* June 7, 2006.

Cole, N. "Understanding Socialization in Sociology" Thought Co. as accessed on Mar 30, 2017: www.thoughtco.com/socialization-in-sociology-4104466

Collins J. and J. Porras. *Built to Last: Successful Habits of Visionary Companies.* New York, HarperCollins, 1994.

Collins J. *Good to Great: Why Some Companies Make the Leap and Others Don't.* New York: HarperCollins, 2001.

Collins, J. "Foreword" *Leadership Lessons from West Point, (Crandall editor),* San Francisco: Wiley, 2006.

Conger, J. *Learning to Lead, the Art of Transforming Managers into Leaders.* San Francisco: Jossey-Bass Publishers, 1992.

Conger, J. and B. Benjamin. *Building Leaders: How Successful Companies Develop the Next Generation.* John Wiley & Sons, 1999.

Conger, J. "Leadership Development Interventions" *Handbook of Leadership Theory and Practice, A Harvard Business School Centennial Colloquium.* Boston: Harvard Business School Press, 2010.

Conger, J. and G. Hollenbeck. "WHAT IS THE CHARACTER OF RESEARCH ON LEADERSHIP CHARACTER?" *Psychology Journal: Practice and Research.* American Psychological Association, December 2010. Vol. 62, No. 4.

Covey, S. *The 7 Habits of Highly Effective People* New York: Simon & Shuster, 1989.

Covey, S. *Principle-Centered Leadership.* New York: Simon & Shuster, 1992.

Cowley, R. and T. Guinzburg. *West Point, Two Centuries of Honor and Tradition.* New York: Warner Books, 2002.

Crossan, M., G. Seijts, and J. Gandz. *Developing Leadership Character.* New York: Taylor & Francis, 2016.

Datar, S., D. Garvin and P. Cullen. *Rethinking the MBA: Business Education at a Crossroads.* Boston: Harvard Business Press, 2010.

Day, D., Harrison, M., & Halpin, S. (2009). *An integrative approach to leader development: connecting adult development, identity and expertise.* [Kindle version]. Retrieved from http://www.amazon.com

Day, D., Zaccaro, S., & Halpin, S. (Eds.). (2007). *Leader development for transforming organizations: growing leaders for tomorrow.* [Kindle version]. Retrieved from http://www.amazon.com

Deal, T. and A. Kennedy. *Corporate Cultures: The Rites and Rituals of Corporate Life.* NY: HarperCollins, 1982.

Deming, W. *Quality, Productivity, and Competitive Position.* Cambridge MA: Massachusetts Institute of Technology, Center for Advanced Engineering Study, 1982.

Dengfeng Zhen, Member of the Chinese Communist Party, in a conversation in Beijing, following his visit to West Point, 2015.

Department of the Army. *The Army Profession (Army Doctrine Reference Publication No. 1)* Washington DC: Headquarters Department of the Army, 14 June 2015.

Department of the Army. *The U.S. Army Leadership Field Manual: FM 6-22* (formerly FM 22-100). Seattle WA: Pacific Publishing Studio, 2011.

DePree, M. *Leadership Jazz.* New York: Dell Publishing, 1992.

Deresiewicz, W. *Excellent Sheep the Miseducation of the American Elite and the Way to a Meaningful Life.* NY: Free Press, 2014.

D'Este, C. *Patton, A Genius for War.* New York: HarperCollins, 1995.

Drucker, P. *The Practice of Management.* New York: HarperCollins, 1990.

Duckworth, A. *Grit: The Power of Passion and Perseverance.* New York: Simon & Schuster, 2016.

Dweck, C. "Student Motivation: What Works, What Doesn't," *Education Week*, Aug 30, 2006.

Eisenhower, D. letter to Maxwell Taylor Jan 2, 1946. West Point Library Archives, West Point, NY.

Fayol, H. *General and Industrial Management 1916.* London: Pitman, 1949.

Fiedler, F. *A Theory of Leadership Effectiveness.* 1967.

Foley, J., J. Hart, and E. Webb. *West Point Sketch Book, USMA Bicentennial Edition* Bloomington IN: Author House, 2004.

Follett, M. *The Creative Experience.* New York: Longmans, Green, 1924.

French, J. and B. Raven. "The Bases of Social Power." *Studies in Social Power*, Dorwin Cartwright (ed.), Research Center for Group Dynamics, Institute for Social Research, University of Michigan, Ann Arbor: 1959.

Gardner J. *On Leadership.* New York: The Free Press, 1993.

Gerras, S. editor *Strategic Leadership Primer 3d ed*, Carlisle Barracks, PA: US Army War College, 2010.

Giber, D., L. Carter, and M. Goldsmith (ed). *Best Practices in Organization and Human Resource Development Handbook: Case Studies, Tools, Models, Research.* Lexington MA: Linkage Inc. 2009.

Goffman, E. *Asylums: Essays on the Social Situation of Mental Patients and Other Inmates.* New York: Random House, 1961.

Grahek, M., A. Thompson, and A. Toliver. "THE CHARACTER TO LEAD: A CLOSER LOOK AT CHARACTER IN LEADERSHIP." *Psychology Journal: Practice and Research.* American Psychological Association, December 2010. Vol. 62, No. 4.

Haidt, J. "The Moral Roots of Liberals and Conservatives." *Tedtalks.* Mar 2008 accessed March 28, 2017 on www.ted.com/talks/jonathan_haidt_on_the_moral_mind?language=en

Hannah, S. and B. Avolio. "MORAL POTENCY: BUILDING THE CAPACITY FOR CHARACTER-BASED LEADERSHIP." *Psychology Journal: Practice and Research.* American Psychological Association, December 2010. Vol. 62, No. 4.

Henley, W. Poem *"Invictus."* (Latin for unconquered) *A Book of Verses.* London: Scribner & Welford, 1891.

Hershey, P. and K. Blanchard. *The Management of Organizational Behavior.* Englewood Cliffs, NJ: Prentice-Hall, 1984.

Herzberg, F., B. Mausner, and B. Snyderman. *The Motivation to Work.* New York: John Wiley & Sons, 1959.

Hickman, J. "Leaders Making Leaders: Crafting Effective Learning Strategies to Promote Army Leadership." Center For Faculty Excellence, West Point NY: United States Military Academy, 2016.

Hogan, R. and J. Hogan. "Assessing Leadership: A View from the Dark Side." *International Journal of Selection and Assessment,* March/June 2001.

Hughes, R., R. Ginnett, and G. Curphy. *Leadership Enhancing the Lessons of Experience 8th edition.* NY: McGraw Hill Education, 2015.

Hymowitz, K. "Is There Anything Grit Can't Do?" Wall Street Journal, June 23, 2017.

Ibarra, H., S. Snook, and L. Ramo. "Identity-Based Leader Development". *Handbook of Leadership Theory and Practice, A Harvard Business School Centennial Colloquium.* Boston: Harvard Business School Press, 2010.

Jamel, K. "Every Graduate a Leader of Character: Character Education at the World's Premier Leader Development Institution." *West Point (Magazine)*, Winter 2017.

Jolly, D. as quoted in D. Brooks. *The Road to Character.* New York: Random House, 2015.

Kaiser, R. and R. Hogan. "HOW TO (AND HOW NOT TO) ASSESS THE INTEGRITY OF MANAGERS." *Psychology Journal: Practice and Research.* American Psychological Association, December 2010. Vol. 62, No. 4.

Katz, D. and R. Kahn. *The Social Psychology of Organizations.* New York: John Wiley and Sons, 1978.

Keenan, M. and B. Sullivan. "Duke Probe Shows Failure of Post-Enron Ethics Classes." *Bloomberg Business.* May 2007.

Kegan, R. *The Evolving Self.* Cambridge, MA: Harvard University Press. 1982.

Kegan, R. *In Over Our Heads: The Mental Demands of Modern Life,* Cambridge, MA: Harvard University Press. 1994.

Kegan, R. and L. Lahey "Adult Development and Organizational Leadership." *Handbook of Leadership Theory and Practice, A Harvard Business School Centennial Colloquium.* Boston: Harvard Business School Press, 2010.

Kellerman, B. *Bad Leadership: What It Is, How It Happens, Why It Matters.* Boston MA: Harvard Business School Press, 2004.

Kellerman, B. *The End of Leadership.* New York: HarperCollins, 2012.

Kennedy, J. *Profiles in Courage.* New York: Harper and Brothers, 1956.

Kennedy, J. and C. Anderson. "Why powerful people fail to stop bad behavior by their underlings; Organizational Behavior and Human Decision Processes." Englewood Sun, March 16, 2017.

Kethledge, R. and M. Erwin "It's Lonely at the Top – or It Should Be." Editorial, *Wall Street Journal:* June 20, 2017.

Khurana, R. *From Higher Aims to Hired Hands,* Princeton: Princeton University Press, 2007.

Khurana, R. and N. Nohria. "It's Time to Make Management a True Profession" *Harvard Business Review*. Boston: Harvard Business School, Oct 2008.

Kolb, D. *Experiential Learning: Experience as the Source of Learning Development*. Englewood Cliffs, New Jersey: Prentice-Hall, Inc., 1984.

Kotter, J. *A Force for Change How Leadership Differs from Management*. New York: The Free Press, 1990.

Kotter, J. *Leading Change*. Boston MA: Harvard Business School Press, 1996.

Kotter, J. *John P. Kotter on What Leaders Really Do*. Boston MA: Harvard Business School Press, 1999.

Kotter, J. and D. Cohen. *The Heart of Change, Real-Life Stories About How People Change Their Organizations*. Boston MA: Harvard Business School Press, 2002.

Kotter, J. and J. Heskett. *Corporate Culture and Performance*. New York: Simon & Schuster, 1992.

Kouzes, J. and B. Posner. *Learning Leadership, the Five Fundamentals of Becoming an Exemplary Leader*. San Francisco: The Leadership Challenge, A Wiley Brand, 2016.

Kouzes, J. and B. Posner, *The Leadership Challenge, How to Get Extraordinary Things Done in Organizations*. San Francisco: Jossey-Bass, 1991.

"Leader Challenge: Company Command, Building Combat-Ready Teams." *Army Magazine*. June 2013.

Leibner, J., G. Mader, and A. Weiss. *The Power of Strategic Commitment*. New York: AMACOM, 2009.

Lencioni, P. "Make Your Values Mean Something." *Harvard Business Review*. Boston: July 2002.

Lewis, T. Chief of Police Punta Gorda, Florida as quoted in *The Englewood Sun*, Nov 6, 2016.

Likert, R. *The Human Organization: Its Management and Value*. New York: McGraw-Hill, 1967.

Lombardo, M. and R. Eichinger. *FYI: For Your Improvement: A Guide for Development and Coaching*. Minneapolis, MN: Lominger Ltd, 2004.

London, J. *Character, The Ultimate Success Factor*. Jacksonville FL: Adducent, Inc., 2013.

Long, L., Principal of Charlotte High School. "Pirates lead, others follow" as quoted in *The Englewood (FL) Sun*, Jan 29, 2016.

Lorsch, J. "A Contingency Theory of Leadership." *Handbook of Leadership Theory and Practice, A Harvard Business School Centennial Colloquium*. Boston: Harvard Business School Press, 2010.

MacDonald, G. "Can business ethics be taught?" *The Christian Science Monitor*, 2007.

Maslow, A. *Motivation and Personality*. New York: Harper and Brothers, 1954.

Maxwell, J. *Developing the Leaders Around You*. Nashville TN: Thomas Nelson, 1995.

Mayo, E. *The Human Problems of an Industrial Civilization*. New York: Viking Press, 1960.

McCain, J. with M. Salter. *Character is Destiny*. New York: Random House, 2005.

McCall, M., M. Lombardo, and A. Morrison. *Lessons of Experience: How Successful Executives Develop on the Job*. New York: Simon & Schuster Inc, 1988.

McCall, M. and G. Hollenbeck. *Developing Global Executives*. Boston: Harvard Business School Press, 2002.

McCauley, C. and C. Douglas. "Developmental Relationships" *The Center for Creative Leadership Handbook of Leadership Development 2d edition*. San Francisco: Jossey-Bass, 2004.

McCauley, C. and E. Van Velsor (editors) *The Center for Creative Leadership Handbook of Leadership Development 2d edition*. San Francisco: Jossey-Bass, 2004.

McDade, S., M. Green. *Investing in Higher Education: A Handbook of Leadership Development*. Phoenix AZ: Onyx Press, 1992.

McDonald, D. *The Golden Passport, Harvard Business School, the limits of capitalism, and the moral failure or the MBA elite.* New York: Harper Collins, 2017.

McDonald, D. "Can You Learn to Lead." *New York Times* April 7, 2015.

McDonald, M. "Dartmouth Gives Students a Lesson: Don't Cheat in Ethics Class." *Bloomberg Business.* Jan 8, 2015.

McGregor, D. *The Human Side of Enterprise.* 1960.

McRaven, W., Admiral US Navy (Retired), Chancellor of the University of Texas System. *Fox News With Chris Wallace.* April 9, 2017.

Murphy, M. *Character Education in America's Blue-Ribbon Schools: Best Practices for Meeting the Challenge.* Lancaster, PA: Technomic Publishing Company, 1998.

Myers, I. B. *Introduction to Type: A Description of the Theory and Applications of the Myers-Briggs Type Indicator* Palo Alto, CA: Consulting Psychologists Press, 1987.

Nohria, N. and R. Khurana. "Advancing Leadership Theory and Practice." *Handbook of Leadership Theory and Practice, A Harvard Business School Centennial Colloquium.* Boston: Harvard Business School Press, 2010.

Nohria, N. and R. Khurana. *Handbook of Leadership Theory and Practice, A Harvard Business School Centennial Colloquium.* Boston: Harvard Business School Press, 2010.

Novotney, A. "Beat the Cheat." American Psychology Association June 2001, Vol 42, No. 6.

OCEAN Model instrument, NEO-IPIP accessed at http://www.personalitytest.net/ipip/ipipneo120.html

Peters, T. and R. Waterman, Jr. *In Search of Excellence.* New York: Harper and Row, 1982.

Pettigrew, A. "On Studying Organizational /Culture," *Administrative Science Quarterly. 24.* 1979

Pfeffer, J. *Leadership BS: Fixing Workplaces and Careers One Truth at a Time.* New York: HarperCollins, 2015.

Pfeffer, J. and R. Sutton. *Hard Facts, Dangerous Half-Truths and Total Nonsense.* Boston: Harvard Business Review Press, 2006.

Plutarch *Lives of the Noble Greeks and Romans* about 100 AD, accessed via https://www.ted.com/speakers/jonathan Jan 20, 2017.

Porter, M. *Competitive Strategy: Techniques for Analyzing Industries and Competitors.* New York: The Free Press, 1980.

Prince, H. "Teaching Leadership: A Journey Into The Unknown." *Concepts and Connections: A Newsletter for Leadership Educators,* Vol. 9 (3); 1, 3, 13; 2001.

Reed, G. "Toxic Leadership." *Military Review*, July-August 2004.

Reeves, R. "The New Politics of Character" *National Affairs* Number 20 – Summer 2014.

Reynolds, S. ed., *Thoughts of Chairman Buffett: Thirty years of Unconventional Wisdom from the Sage of Omaha.* New York: Harper Business, 2011.

Riggio, R., W. Zhu, C. Reina, and J. Maroosis. "VIRTUE-BASED MEASUREMENT OF ETHICAL LEADERSHIP: THE LEADERSHIP VIRTUES QUESTIONNAIRE" *Psychology Journal: Practice and Research.* American Psychological Association, December 2010. Vol. 62, No. 4.

Schaeffer, F. "My Heart on the Line." *The Washington Post,* Nov 26, 2002.

Schein, E. with P. Schein. *Organizational Culture and Leadership 5th Edition.* Hoboken NJ: John Wiley &Sons. 2017. (first edition 1985)

Selznick, P. *Leadership in Administration, A Sociological Interpretation.* New York: Harper & Row, 1957.

Senn, L. and J. Childress. *The Secret of a Winning Culture.* Los Angeles, CA: Leadership Press, 1999.

Shields, C., "Aristotle's Philosophical Life and Writings." *The Oxford Handbook of Aristotle.* New York: Oxford University Press, 2012.

Snider, D. and L. Matthews. *The Future of the Army Profession 2d edition.* Boston: McGraw-Hill, 2002.

Star Wars. *"The Empire Strikes Back."* 1980 American epic space opera film.

Stogdill, F. *Handbook of Leadership: A Survey of Theory and Research.* New York, NY: Free Press, 1974.

"Strong's Concordance 5481" *NAS Exhaustive Concordance of the Bible with Hebrew-Aramaic and Greek Dictionaries*, The Lockman Foundation, 1998.

Sturm, R., D. Vera, and M. Crossan. "The entanglement of leader character and leader competence and its impact on performance." *The Leadership Quarterly.* 28 (2017).

Taylor, F. *The Principles of Scientific Management.* New York: Harper and Brothers, 1911.

Tennyson, A. "The Charge of the Light Brigade." As accessed on June 4, 2017 at www.poetry.eserver.org/light-brigade.html

Tichy, N. and M. DeVanna, *The Cycle of Leadership: How Great Leaders Teach Their Companies to Win.* New York: Harper Collins, 1986.

Tichy, N. and E. Cohen. *The Leadership Engine: How Winning Companies Build Leaders at Every Level.* New York: Harper Collins, 1997.

Thompson, A. and R. Riggio. "Special Issue on Defining and Measuring Character in Leadership." *Psychology Journal: Practice and Research.* American Psychological Association, December 2010. Vol. 62, No. 4.

Ulmer W. "Toxic Leadership, What Are We Talking About." *Army Magazine*, June 2012.

Van Maanen, J. and E. Schein "Toward a Theory of Organizational Socialization." *Research in Organizational Behavior.* Vol. 1. Greenwich CT: JAI Press, 1979.

Van Velsor, E., R. Moxley, and K. Bunker. "The Leader Development Process." *The Center for Creative Leadership Handbook of Leadership Development 2d edition.* San Francisco: Jossey-Bass, 2004.

Van Velsor, E. and W. Drath. "A Lifelong Developmental Perspective on Leader Development." *The Center for Creative Leadership Handbook of Leadership Development 2d edition.* San Francisco: Jossey-Bass, 2004.

Weber, M. *The Protestant Ethic and the Spirit of Capitalism.* New York: Routledge Classics, 1930.

Weber, M. *Economy and Society: An Outline of Interpretative Sociology.* New York: Bedminster Press, 1968.

"West Point." A magazine of the West Point Association of Graduates. West Point NY, Spring 2017.

"West Point." A magazine of the West Point Association of Graduates. West Point NY, Winter 2017.

West Point annual publication, *Bugle Notes.* West Point NY: United States Military Academy Library, Years, 1950-2016.

West Point Course Syllabus, MX 400 Officership. West Point NY: United States Military Academy, 2017.

West Point Document, Cadet Leader Development System (CLDS) West Point NY: United States Military Academy, 2008.

West Point Pamphlet. *Building Capacity to Lead, the West Point System for Leader Development.* West Point NY: United States Military Academy, 2009.

West Point Pamphlet. *Character Development Strategy, Live Honorably and Build Trust.*

West Point NY: United States Military Academy, December 2014.

West Point Pamphlet. *USCC Pamphlet 15-1. The Cadet Honor Code, System, and Committee Procedures.* West Point NY: Headquarters United States Corps of Cadets, 9 October 2015.

West Point Pamphlet. *USMA Character Program (Gold Book).* West Point NY: United States Military Academy, May 2015.

West Point Pamphlet. *West Point Leader Development System.* West Point NY: United States Military Academy, 2015.

"What Price Honor? The West Point Scandal." *Time Magazine.* June 7, 1976.

Wolf, R. "Government upbraided in stripped citizenship case." *USA Today.* June 23, 2017.

Yukl, G. *Leadership in Organizations 8th Ed.* Upper Saddle River, NJ: Pearson/Prentice Hall, 2013.

Zenger, J. "We Wait Too Long to Train Our Leaders." *Harvard Business Review.* Dec 17, 2012.

Zalesnik A. *Human Dilemmas of Leadership.* New York: Harper & Row, 1966.

Zalesnik A. "Managers and Leaders: Are They Different?" *Harvard Business Review, 1977.*

Websites:

www.ed.gov

www.hbs.edu

www.pwc.com

www.amanet.org

www.universityworldnews.com

www.forbes.com

www.ted.com/speakers

www.ted.com/talks/jonathan_haidt

www.viacharacter.org/viainstitute/classification.aspx

www.kconnection.com/character+competence-sa

www.sigmaassessmentsystems.com

www.andersonleadershipsolutions.com/character-test/

www.stockfuse.com

www.nack.it.com

www.pymetrics.com

www.tycoonsystems.com

www.alibabagroup.com/en/about/culture

www.en.wikipedia.org/wiki/McDonald's

www.en.wikipedia.org/wiki/Master_of_Business_Administration#History

www.en.wikipedia.org/wiki/List_of_business_schools_in_the_United_States

www.iep.utm.edu/cicero/

www.thoughtco.com/socialization-in-sociology-4104466

Robert C. Carroll
Colonel, US Army (Retired)
Unparalleled experience in the leadership field

| 1983 | 2017 |

Military	Civilian
Student of Leadership	
- West Point BS - Ranger School - Infantry Officer Courses - Air Force Staff College	- Northwestern MA; Auburn MPA - Harvard Business School AMP - Aspen Institute for Ethics - Center for Creative Leadership
Experience as a Leader	
- Platoon and Company Command in Hawaii and Vietnam. - Battalion Command in Colorado and Germany.	- VP Human Resources then Division President, Goldome Savings Bank; - SVP, Bank One Youngstown.
Teacher of Leadership	
- To cadets at West Point; - To Commanders and Command Sergeants Major at Army posts across the US.	- To executives and senior Management teams in the US, Canada, the UK, Japan, and China.
Program Management of Leadership	
- In charge of leadership policy for the US Army, as Chief, Leadership Division, in the Pentagon.	- Consulted with corporate leaders in the US, Canada, the UK, and Japan on enhancing their leader development programs.

The author resides on Manasota Key in Englewood, Florida.
His interests include bicycling and tap dancing.
www.buildingyourleadershiplegacy.com

Made in the USA
Columbia, SC
20 February 2018